PRAISE FOR *SPIRITUAL*

T0023227

'Ilana's important work here illustra
and it is soul food for grounding,
spiritual core. There are so many un............ ...y presented
that our society needs to hear. May her words touch your spirit as they
have mine.'

MAEGAN COKER, SPIRITUAL MEDIUM & INTUITIVE

'Spirituality enables us as souls within a physical body to examine our
experiences and in how we deal with them. The soul is never limited
by the physical body, nor by any imperfections. How we as sentient
beings overcome any physical limitation or disability, shows the soul's
determination to grow and continue on its pathway, having a disability
within the physical aspect of a soul's journey; the impact, the limitations,
the discrimination. This wonderful book highlights the importance of
having a spiritual belief in one's life journey, in encompassing the
role spirituality has in our individual life and its unique role upon
our life journeys. I am happy to bless this book throughout and give
my spiritualist medium blessings to both the author and reader, in
encouraging any individual within a similar position, to utilise the power
and the importance of spirituality in assisting you on your pathway.'

CHRISTOPHER CRAIG HUNT-LAW, SPIRITUALIST MEDIUM

'I could not put this epic story down, finally a book that helps us to
understand the process some experience during healing and growing.
Inspirational and beautiful.'

BRYAN BENSON, SPIRITUAL GUIDE AND PSYCHIC COUNSEL

'Experience has taught me that many will travel their entire journey
having never realised the spiritual elements involved in their healing.
Ilana Estelle is definitely not one of those people and I've very much
enjoyed reading about the insight she's gleaned from her powerful
journey. This is a wonderful story of survival and personal development
and I recommend it to anyone who finds themselves seeking.'

LAWSON PATTERSON, PSYCHIC ADVISOR, MEDIUM, TEACHER, COUNSEL

'Everyone has something they've read or listened to, which makes a lifetime impression. It may only be a paragraph or one line that replays in your mind. Yet you carry it with you. There are plenty of these moments in this easy-to-read book.'

SARAH TUESDAY HATHOR, INTUITIVE CONSULTANT

'Ilana touched on my own spiritual journey with my own chronic illness. Reading this book was like having a conversation with an old friend who offers you a comforting hug and guidance towards spiritual healing. It is a reminder that you aren't alone even if you feel as though you are. It will help you find that essential source of self-love and self-compassion we all need when dealing with our everyday baggage.'

MARIA THE ARCANE

'Once again, Ilana Estelle shoots straight from the heart and hits her mark. With a unique blend of pragmatism and spiritual insight she lays down principles of inner healing that are both time-honoured and fresh. Ilana's wisdom did not come without a price; it was born from severe adversity. Her most recent book, *Spirituality, Healing and Me*, is a gift to the universe.'

TR BAUER, AUTHOR AND ACTIVIST

'Ilana makes spirituality deeply personal in her book *Spirituality, Healing, and Me*. Her journey to spirituality is more than just a coping mechanism to thrive despite her medical condition. She adopted it as a way of life to truly experience and appreciate what is unfolding right before her eyes. If you want to be inspired and learn more about your own personal relationship with spirituality, then this book is for you.'

MAI CADIZ, BOOK REVIEWER

'*Spirituality, Healing and Me*, is a reference guide on how to survive life. Ilana places her readers in the path of their full potential, so that they may find true enlightenment. I saw all aspects of myself on every page.'

TIM LEE, READER REVIEW

'Most of us have had certain books in our lifetime that we have returned to over and over again. Unquestionably, *Cerebral Palsy – A Story* is destined to become one of those books. Written by Ilana Estelle in a style that is comprehensive and, unlike many books about self-awareness discovery and wisdom that typically include flowery wording and no shortage of fluff, this book, refreshingly, is straightforward and tells it like it is.

Like your favourite soulmate, lifelong friend, or political favourite who will never quite make it to the top, this insightful book is, simply, good through and through.

Without being preachy, Ilana takes us on her life's journey, leaving no stone unturned, and includes perfectly placed, potent quotes along the way from notable personalities such as the Dalai Lama, John Lennon, Winston Churchill, Rumi and more.

This is a book you'll want to loan out to people you care about. May the laws of attraction work their magic; and may this important and inspiring book help bring a greater sense of clarity and balance to everyone who reads it'

MARTY KINROSE, FORMER DIRECTOR OF MENTOR AND YOUTH
PROGRAMS AT UCP WORK INC.

'*Cerebral Palsy – A Story* is not only enlightening; it is an honest to God original piece of work… This book is a lifeline for anyone who has endured hardship on this great voyage we call life. It is my hope that Ilana's teachings will help you as much as they have helped me'

TR BAUER, AUTHOR & ACTIVIST

READER REVIEWS

'Five inspirational stars for a read that will make you cry, give you hope, and cheer for the courage of this magnificent woman'

'This book is a must read for anyone struggling with personal life challenges… it resonated with me on a deep level and while I do not have cerebral palsy, we can all relate to the challenges she takes on with a mature and retrospective lens'

'This book is a spiritually driven masterpiece. A story of triumph through struggle and pain. I found myself riveted on every page. I will reference this book forever'

'I found it a fascinating and very readable book, with some very interesting thoughts. It is an intensely honest book, which I found genuinely interesting throughout... It adds greatly to the understanding of the effects of late diagnosis, and the effects of autism in one life'

'These words are powerful, inspiring, and most importantly – doable... This book is not your typical self-help or inspirational book'

'Thank you for such a great read! I now want to know details about her life, what it is like for her to be a mother, and much more. I hope she writes an autobiography!'

'I really enjoyed reading this book... The style is gentle and easy to read... It is not just for people living with a disability – there is wisdom here for all of us'

'An inspirational read, which is not just for people with cerebral palsy, but for anybody who has had to face challenges in their life'

'The incredible story is about how positive thinking, healthy eating and mindfulness can change your life for the better. Highly recommended'

'It is a beautifully written book full of her personal story, medical facts and so much more'

'I found the book very inspirational, a great story of overcoming challenges through life, well written and easy to read'

'Her story is both an inspiration and an education, with valuable advice and lessons in life… I highly recommend this book – it's a must read'

'Truly a book for all people. If you have faced adversity or sought to understand yourself and your situation better, there is something for you in this book'

'Ilana's story is astonishing, compelling and truly inspiring. You will have missed a trick, if you don't read it! This book will and should changes lives'

'This book is brilliant… if you're looking for a story about an inspiring woman who has overcome a lot in her life and come out of the other side still smiling and stronger than ever then this is the one for you'

'The book is insightful, sometimes painful to read, but most of all an inspiring account of a woman's journey to find her true self and understand her own disabilities in an able world'

'An inspiring story'

'An inspiring story of a woman who struggled through adversity and educated herself to the point of guiding others through their own struggles… I thoroughly enjoyed her book. A good read'

'Very very inspirational – never, never let your imperfections define you'

Join the conversation at
www.thecpdiary.com

ILANA ESTELLE

SPIRITUALITY, HEALING AND ME

How Living a Spiritual Life
Offers Hope and Healing
in the Modern World

Red Door

Published by RedDoor
www.reddoorpress.co.uk

The right of Ilana Estelle to be identified as author of this Work has
been asserted by her in accordance with sections 77 and 78 of the
Copyright, Designs and Patents Act 1988

978-1-913062-66-8

A CIP catalogue record for this book is available from the British
Library

Cover design: Emily Courdelle

Typesetting: Jen Parker, Fuzzy Flamingo
www.fuzzyflamingo.co.uk

Printed and bound in Denmark by Nørhaven

This book is dedicated to those trying to heal in a confusing world;
may you see the light

CONTENTS

FOREWORD

My first introduction into spirituality and healing was when I finally decided it was time for me to stop ignoring the paranormal phenomena that had occurred around me for as long as I could remember. I taught myself to meditate in hopes of connecting with someone beyond this earthly plane who by chance might help me to understand the phenomena I experienced daily. Much to my surprise the result had nothing to do with connecting to the other world and everything to do with learning about the real me. I healed from the inside out and set out on my own spiritual journey.

I eventually ended up at the prestigious Author Findlay College in Stansted, England where I studied for the next six years to become a medium. I learned there the importance of going within to heal, discovered the spiritual being I am and finally after fifty years of living, I began to understand all I had been through in this lifetime. It was life changing.

I was delighted and honoured when Ilana Estelle contacted me to write the foreword to her book *Spirituality, Healing and Me*. I know all too well the impact of finding your own spiritual path to heal from within.

In her first book, *Cerebral Palsy – A Story: Finding the*

Calm After the Storm, author Ilana Estelle brilliantly paints a picture of her struggle, pain and courage growing up. She invites the reader along on her journey of self-awareness and discovery as she delved into the soul of her true essence and understanding her life with cerebral palsy.

In her newest masterpiece, *Spirituality, Healing and Me*, Ilana not only takes you with her on her spiritual journey of healing she takes the time to explain what she's experiencing, how it helped her and how you can do the same. She shares her story – a story of healing, triumph and determination inspiring the reader to do the same.

Ilana gives you the tools to overcome the adversities you may have in your own life. She lifts your spirit and shows you the possibilities of healing the trauma from the past or moving through your current difficulties.

The reader will walk away inspired, uplifted, and full of hope.

Ilana has walked this path. She discovered self-healing while on her quest to understand her own body, thoughts, and emotions. She found Ilana. The real Ilana. The warrior goddess Ilana of strength, courage, and determination that was there all along waiting to step forward.

If you have experienced trauma or are currently going through a tough time, read this book! Let Ilana guide you to discovering your true self and set you free on your own spiritual path. Ilana was able to find her own calm after the storm and this book can help you find your calm.

KAY REYNOLDS, author of *The Evidential Medium: A Practical Guide for Developing Mediumship*

INTRODUCTION

As a small child growing up, my only concern was putting a name to something I didn't know I had. As the years went by, the thought never left me that going to the grave without knowing was always a distinct possibility. Even if I had a diagnosis back then, there would have been more to it than just the label.

I wrote about this in my first book, *Cerebral Palsy: A Story, Finding the Calm After the Storm*. Some people might find it difficult to comprehend that I never understood what my disability was, or what having a bad leg or foot meant, or why I wasn't told. Having lived with a disability I didn't know anything about growing up, those were my thoughts too. Even today, I struggle to comprehend the time span and enormity of not knowing.

After I found out I had cerebral palsy, it was important I didn't continue to focus on what I saw as negative. I wanted to do something positive for the first time. I started writing because it was a positive thing to do after such a late cerebral palsy diagnosis. I needed and wanted to learn about my physical, mental and emotional difficulties. I wanted to understand. I also wanted to change what I knew about myself. I was starting from scratch. It was important to me that I was able to make sense of and change my experiences moving forward, so that I could finally bring closure on my disability.

I've had to piece my life together bit by bit. I've also had to learn about my disability and that has taken time. Through the process, I wanted to understand and to get to know 'me', but my journey has turned out to be so much more. Writing allows me to talk about my experiences, so that I can go on to make sense of my life's experiences.

My first book was about living with a disability that I didn't know I had and finding out at forty-six that I had been diagnosed aged two. It was my story, encompassing my thoughts and feelings from childhood, through my adult years, and the present day. My spiritual beliefs helped me through those difficult times.

This, my second book, is themed in exactly the same way, following on from my first. It is structured as a collection of reflections arranged in chapters, around themes. Some chapters continue to unfold my thoughts, feelings and experiences, while others provide an insight into my spirituality and healing that have allowed me to move forward with my life, through a more positive outlook. Although I touched on spirituality and healing in my first book, I didn't incorporate either in their wider context.

I don't know how old I was when I began to realise that having physical issues meant there would be a question mark over my long-term emotional and physical health. Although I didn't understand because I didn't know I had a disability, I was sure I needed to wise up.

When I was young, I was already beginning to think about spirituality. Although I wasn't quite sure what it meant in its wider context that would come later, I was innately aware of a connection, a driving force connecting me to something bigger. I also wasn't sure how it would help me in my life, but I was sure it was something I needed to explore further.

Being spiritual is universal, something that, when embraced, can help us find peace. It is a lifestyle choice that allows us to think about our place in the world. It helps us to flourish as individuals, it gives us a purpose and brings meaning into our lives. It promotes emotional and physical well-being and raises our self-esteem and confidence.

Being spiritual also helps us strive towards a better life. It promotes physical, emotional and spiritual growth. It helps us focus on our internal values and helps us become better people.

It promotes personal healing and positive emotions associated with the smaller pleasures in life. Spirituality keeps us grounded, more humbled and allows us to appreciate our lives and each other more.

Our starting point for spiritual growth is the point where we find out about ourselves. The moment we start to look at ourselves more closely will always be the catalyst for a change in attitude from us. I innately knew that whatever I was dealing with as a child, spirituality and healing would eventually play a big part in my life. I am now passionate about both.

Knowing and understanding what we deal with is the

start of any healing process. It is not enough to ignore the fact that we deal with something; or settle into life without attempting to deal with it. It is important we find ways to manage things.

It is important we come to know and understand ourselves, so that we can incorporate a better lifestyle around our issues. Through a better lifestyle, we should be able to manage our concerns with a little more ease. It will always be better for us, if we learn to co-exist and manage what we deal with.

Embracing spirituality and a better lifestyle have been the catalyst to an open door for me, leading me into a world of writing that goes beyond what I might have otherwise been able to achieve. I am thankful for both the opportunity and the gift.

CHAPTER 1

WHAT IS SPIRITUALITY?

'The great awareness comes slowly, piece by piece. The path of spiritual growth is a path of lifelong learning. The experience of spiritual power is basically a joyful one.'

M. SCOTT PECK

Spirituality is the state, or fact of being spiritual. In the broader context, it includes a sense of connection to something that is bigger than us.

Spirituality and a spiritual belief system are incredibly helpful for coping with unprecedented and challenging times. On a day-to-day basis, it helps me cope with the challenges I face in this ever-changing world. My beliefs have helped me through the most difficult of times.

How spiritual you are depends on how willing you are to make the connections between your emotional and spiritual health. Being spiritual helps us navigate through our lives, so that the road ahead isn't as bumpy as it might otherwise be. When we behave in ways that are spiritual, our suffering and struggles become less.

Spirituality has very little to do with religion. It is simply a measure of how kind and loving we are, how accepting we are towards ourselves and towards others, and how compassionate, empathetic and tolerant we are as people. We don't have to look outwards to find spirituality; it is something that is in all of us.

SPIRITUALITY AND ME

I never tire of writing about, or wanting to learn more about spirituality, because it has brought a certain calm to my life.

Spirituality has given me the power to choose how I see and create my own realities. It has shown me that my life reflects what I put out into the world. When others think the same way, it is like meeting someone for the first time and realising how much we have in common.

When we begin to take an interest in the universe, we begin to understand the bigger picture, how spirituality ties us to the universe and to each other and where our lives fit in; when we want to know how it all works, asking questions like, 'What is my purpose?' and 'Where did we come from?' we know we're beginning to understand the spiritual concept, and what it means to be 'spiritual'.

When we begin to show qualities such as respect, tolerance, and understanding for others, we know we're on the spiritual path. Spirituality brings meaning to our lives, and how to get the best out of what we have. It is open to everyone.

UNDERSTANDING SPIRITUALITY

Spirituality is not always fully understood. For those like me who are spiritual, but not religious, we may reject traditional organised religion.

Being spiritual is not the same as being religious. Religion is about worship, a system of belief, and involves a code of ethics and believing in a god. Religion is something *found*.

Spirituality is the quality of *being* spiritual, a non-physical presence shown in life, in thought. Spirituality is innate, it is in each of us. We encounter spirituality when we wonder and question where the universe comes from, why we are here, what happens when we die, and when we think about the universe and how our lives fit into that. Spirituality is also part of the healing process.

Being spiritual means we focus on the spiritual world as opposed to earthly and physical things. Being decent human beings, how we behave, and what we have to offer as individuals through spirituality is extremely important.

Spirituality exists where we may struggle with the complexities of how our lives fit into the greater universe. When our personal values become bigger and more important than our religious values, we are spiritual.

If, like me, your values include empathy, compassion, tolerance and patience that reveal a power beyond the visible world, you know you are spiritual. It is something we can all be.

When you are ready to establish and learn about the powers governing the universe and your life, you know you're on a spiritual path.

ETHICAL PRINCIPLES

Ethical principles are a philosophical stance which directly or indirectly leads to a standard based around ethics.

Ethics means 'moral principles that govern a person or group's behaviour'.

The four principles of ethics are:

INTEGRITY

To behave in accordance with ethical principles, act in honesty, fairness and in good faith.

IMPARTIALITY AND INDEPENDENCE

To remain impartial and to conduct oneself in the interests of others and to ensure that any personal views and convictions do not compromise ethical principles, or official duties.

ACCOUNTABILITY

To take responsibility for one's decisions, actions and their consequences.

RESPECT

To continue to respect the diversity, equality, dignity, worth and privacy of all people. We should at all times promote a high level of professionalism towards decisions and actions to make sure these are upheld, through mandates and objectives.

For those who are in a place of power and have responsibility, it is even more important they remain impartial. Others are relying on them to get that right, whether it's in politics, in business or through an institution.

For society and the world to live in sync and in harmony with each other, it is important we all live by the same rules. (Source: https://www.who.int)

PARALLEL LIVES

As a young adult, I used to see the passing of someone as a final gesture, not something that was an extension of where they had already come from: the spirit world. Before we're born into this life, I believe we come from spirit and have lived other lives. As we prepare to say our goodbyes, those waiting to make the transition go back to the spirit world and live a life parallel to ours.

Death, which may seem taboo to some and final to others, should be neither. Where their life is complete this side of life, they continue their lives in spirit, just not here with us.

THE UNIVERSAL TRUTH

You could say that a truth is 'universal' if it is irrefutably valid and logical, so a universal truth is impossible to deny, and it is the same for everyone. For example, everything we do starts with a single thought.

Some of us may live our lives in denial about what are the universal truths. Perhaps we're in denial because it's easier; or perhaps we're aware the truth may open wounds that are easier left unopened. Perhaps it's not you, perhaps it's someone else who is denying the truth, because they know that what they're doing is something the universe won't agree to.

But whatever our reasons for ignoring the truth, it can never bring the right choices, or the right outcomes. When anyone ignores the universal truth, not only can it hurt them, it can also change the family dynamics as that person continues to gloss over it. And as hard as it is to be honest and upfront, what we tell others is important, because it not only shapes us as individuals, our lives and our children's lives, it's also a conversation with the universe.

I am aware that without my writing, I would be no nearer to understanding my truth, or my disabilities. I certainly wouldn't have gone down the 'knowing what I have' route.

But if like me, you believe in the universe, and the universal truths and you believe life turns out the way it is meant to, it would always have taken me this long to get to everything I've had to deal with and achieve. Put simply, my experiences to the point of diagnosis of cerebral palsy at forty-six, and my autism diagnosis at fifty-six, were my experiences to have.

For us to continue to encourage positive thinking, self-confidence and a positive outlook, it is important to bring universal truths into the equation around our experiences and find an acceptance on those.

No matter how long it takes to accept our truth, the universal truth always prevails and acts and just because we are in denial or ignore it, that doesn't mean the universe has its blinkers on. The universe knows our truth and it is not something we can avoid. Things have a way of coming back to us, everyone is accountable.

THE PSYCHE

The psyche is the totality of the human mind, conscious and unconscious. It represents one of the fundamental concepts for understanding human nature. The psyche is the driving force behind our personality traits and behind our characters. Together they make up our personalities.

Because much of our thinking and behaviour is driven by our beliefs, habits, attitudes, and assumptions that are so deep in our psyche, we are not always fully aware of them.

It is the unconscious part of our brain that communicates with the conscious and it is that which provides us with the meaning to all our interactions with the world, as filtered through our beliefs and habits. The psyche communicates through feelings, imagination, emotions, dreams and sensations.

The psyche defines us, our characters, how we are and how we behave. In our personal journey of self-understanding and emotional growth, it is important we explore our psyche, to understand why we may appear a certain way. Once we're aware of our psyche, we can work to change those aspects of our character and behaviour that we feel needs changing.

The psyche knows everything about us. It knows if we're being stubborn, or inconsiderate, it knows when we're kind and caring, it knows if we're moody. The psyche knows us more than we know ourselves, because it lies deep within our unconscious and *is* us. But unless we know how to tap into our unconscious and connect with our psyche, nothing within us can ever change.

The psyche is our personal coding to just about everything. Tapping into our psyche allows us to change certain aspects of our personality for the better.

OUR BELIEF SYSTEM

We all have a belief system that affects how we live day to day. Over time that belief system may begin to affect how we perceive and interpret what we see, feel and hear.

If we continually live with negativity, our belief system may eventually begin to see all our past, present and future situations in negative ways. It takes work for us to identify the beliefs that begin to affect our lives negatively. Through our beliefs, we can learn to identify and release ourselves from any negative thoughts.

The more we work on our feelings and beliefs, the more peace we can have in the longer term. Feelings remain inside of us until we learn how to challenge, direct and change them. We may replicate the same feelings and emotions we have in childhood in our adult life. We may also take our feelings and emotions with us.

It's commonly believed that if we change our circumstances, we can be happier, but we need to think about and work on ourselves first for change to happen. That said, we can always change how we see our perceptions and behaviour, so that we see the positive and act on that.

MORE ON SPIRITUALITY

It is said by some that religion and spirituality are total opposites. Historically, we were spiritual, long before we found religion. Religion is associated with the concerns of a life through faith, culture and society.

Spirituality is described as an attachment to one's inner soul through life and how we choose to live it. It allows us to look at a wealth of opportunities, so that we may live life in its simplest form.

When you can accept yourself emotionally, physically and spiritually, you know you're on the spiritual path. The spiritual path allows us to accept the things we cannot change, deal with the things we can and give of ourselves, without needing anything in return.

It's not something that just happens, it's a journey of different experiences, culminating in emotional tranquillity and peace that comes from within, allowing us to choose how we see other people and the world. It sets us apart from others, through our attitude and behaviour.

Spirituality helps us understand ourselves, our lives and others, and that puts us in tune with ourselves and our lives.

AN AWAKENING

An awakening is when you become aware of something, you make a connection for the first time. It is a realisation, or a recognition.

Not everyone experiences an awakening, but anyone who has an awakening, knows it's there. It may not be something you personally experience, it can be something you learn about through someone else, or something you come to understand through spiritual growth.

It's something you can intuitively come to know about. It's a process where your eyes are opened after having had them shut for so long. It's also a process where you can see things for the first time, that you couldn't or didn't see; or something you were avoiding that needed to be addressed.

Through an awakening, you experience life and the people in your lives in a totally different way. For the first time, you're looking at people without rose-coloured spectacles and that can feel overwhelming.

It's when you start looking at something in the whole, like the colours of the flowers, or you notice the birds singing for the very first time. Noticing and seeing people's true colours can also be an awakening.

It is a new energy, working on a higher frequency, a realisation that can be quite refreshing for some, but overwhelming for others. An awakening is an important change we can all learn to embrace. It is a change easy to resist, but resisting simply causes pressure to build and that can leave you feeling overwhelmed.

Working on a higher frequency takes practice; the more you deal with how you feel, the less overwhelmed you should feel.

WHEN SOULS CONNECT

The soul is what we have in common, and yet we can spend a lifetime in relationships thinking we have nothing in common with the people we share our lives with.

We may think our relationships aren't working because we have nothing in common, but it's not always about that. Relationships connect through the soul. If you are with the right person, you know because your souls connect.

Relationships and friendships are less stressful when two souls connect on a level far greater than what we see physically, on the outside. When souls connect, you don't have to try too hard.

Away from the soul we should continue to work on our relationships; listen more attentively, communicate and be prepared to continue making those emotional connections. Sounds obvious, but it's not as obvious as you think. We may become complacent; we don't always try, or make the effort.

When souls connect, we already have that in common. Unfortunately, when we place too much value on material worth, we may fail to see, or work on our connections. Relationships need empathy, compassion and tolerance.

Sadly, with all that is happening in the world, we in fact have the opposite. But by making others a priority and being attentive, relationships can work, even without the soulful connections.

A SOULFUL CONNECTION

We have a mind, physical body and soul. Although our lives start in the physical form when we're born, we have already had past lives, some with people we're in contact with in our current life, and some people we've yet to meet.

Have you ever had a fleeting moment where you meet someone for the first time, and you get that feeling that you know them? That feeling comes from the soul. Some souls may feel as though they already know each other, other souls may feel at ease in each other's company and some other souls may clash.

As we journey through life, some souls we come across may help us grow in wisdom and love, other souls may help us learn difficult lessons and universal truths, and other souls we come across may not teach us anything at all. That is because they're not learning their own lessons, so have nothing to impart on us. When that happens, it is likely that we may have something to teach them.

But it is up to each of us to learn and understand how the soul works. When we choose not to learn, we get caught up in earthly trappings that take us away from our lessons and our understanding of how the soul works. The lessons we acquire through the soul automatically concur with the universe and how the universe works.

The connection we get from that 'just knowing' feeling is from our karmic past. It is a past shared history connection, catching up with us in this life.

THE CYCLE OF LIFE

The mere thought of death can send shivers down our spines, it's a subject that has been taboo for far too long.

We talk about life, but we fail to talk about death in the same way, and considering death is our only surety, it is tragic that we cannot bring ourselves to discuss it.

Death is part of life, and without experiencing life to its fullest, we're more likely to avoid, or try to postpone the experience of death. Fearing death means fearing what could in effect be our most important experience.

Instead, we should talk about death and bring it back into our everyday. We should also talk about the people we have loved and lost. After all, they lived, they were part of our lives and yet we sometimes find it difficult to talk about them.

My own belief is that without death, life is incomplete. Life is a cycle, and death is part of that cycle. It is a process and being born is part of the same process. We don't remember being born, but we're here. It's something we've experienced, so we should perhaps contemplate death in the same way.

Death is inevitable. We need to understand and be comfortable with the idea and its concept, because fearing it only limits our ability to make the most of the life we have. In my twenties, the thought of death scared me 'half to death'. Now, spirituality is the closest belief system I know that allows me to understand the concepts of life and death perfectly.

In effect, we are all spiritual beings living a spiritual experience, whether we believe in the spiritual concept or not. Death is part of that same experience.

DEEP UNDERSTANDING

It is important we have a deep understanding of our lives. From around the age of nine or ten, I was already putting some of the pieces of my life together. Innately, my spiritual beliefs were already there, but my deeper understanding of spirituality would come later.

Although we may have a deep understanding of our lives; we may not always be ready, or in a position to change it. What is important is that we have understanding, because without that, nothing can change.

With deep understanding we recognise the essence of something; in other words, the basic and most important characteristic, which gives its individual identity. When we make sense of something, our understanding is deepened, and the information we gain can be used in new ways to change the way we see our issues, situation and circumstances.

Deep understanding allows us to reason with what we know and with what we can comprehend and change. Through spiritual and emotional growth, we can choose not to hold on to the things that no longer serve us.

Having a deep understanding helps us to stop making premature judgments. It also helps us enhance our relationships, which in turn brings about healthier outcomes.

SPIRITUAL & EMOTIONAL GROWTH

When we fail to open our minds to the possibilities of what we can learn and how we can change, we inhibit spiritual and emotional growth and as a consequence may fail to move forward, or understand how we could have contributed to our circumstances differently.

Just because we grow older, doesn't mean we grow wiser, more mature, or attain spiritual growth. As we continue life's journey, we may go through sequences that test our abilities to listen, and express ourselves, it's important not to give up.

The very nature of an experience allows us the opportunity to heal and grow, but for this to be successful we should continue to work through our experiences. A part of spiritual growth is about learning to release the emotions that weigh heavily, the exact emotions we need to let go of, particularly if we can't secure a desired outcome. We need to learn and understand when it is time to let go.

The emotional release as the process resolves itself can leave us feeling more alive, less anxious and irritated, less fearful and free without attachments, allowing us to stay presently focused. Spiritual and emotional growth is cumulative and needs to be continually worked on, so that we can build on our emotional strength.

Whether it happens quickly or slowly can depend on the individual, but we can't evolve without it. When we understand our attachments and why it's important to let go of them, we can have peace. To do that, we need clarity around our perceptions. In fact, it is only when we can look back at something from our past and we're feeling okay about it that we know we are healed.

Mental clarity associated with emotional healing may foster wisdom; wisdom may foster compassion; compassion may foster understanding; understanding may foster tolerance and selflessness to accept why we are where we are.

When we are able to accept a loss through a relationship, through a death, or through the loss of a pet and we are able to weather the storm, and calm can finally be restored, then we may achieve emotional and spiritual growth.

LESSONS IN DIFFICULT TIMES

We learn our lessons in the most difficult of times and this is a necessary part of spiritual and emotional growth. It is only through difficult times that we learn how to become adept at dealing with, and working through our experiences. I come back to resilience, because the more resilient we are, the stronger we are to get through tough times.

Although resilience can help us bounce back, it cannot guarantee us a life without stress. Instead, resilience helps us to focus, so that we can learn how to equate what we see and understand.

In fact, it is only through understanding that we learn our biggest lessons, helping us to create new opportunities. Through new opportunities we gain new thinking; through new thinking, we acquire more knowledge and through more knowledge, we learn how to manage our stress.

When we learn how to manage our stress, we become more adept at changing our perceptions of it. With our changing perceptions, we can learn our lessons, even in difficult times. Lessons are necessary for spiritual and emotional growth.

ISSUES ARE LESSONS

I believe the issues we deal with are our lessons in life and that if we were to stand back and look at those issues, we would see and understand how we could do things differently.

I work on my own understanding that issues are obstacles, challenges and problems that we may initiate ourselves, often without understanding. If we work on the understanding that everything that happens to us happens for a reason, and that issues are lessons, once we learn how to understand those lessons, we can find the answers that resolve our issues.

Too often we get caught up in internal dialogue and ask why things happen to us. The worst part of any scenario is the internal dialogue that comes with it, that and the inevitable wallowing in self-pity. Unfortunately, we may spend too much time dwelling on our issues, instead of trying to find out how we can best address them. It's a human failing, but one that is easily remedied with a positive attitude.

In my own case, I innately knew my physical difficulties were there for a reason. Years later I would understand why.

We can learn so much from the cards we're dealt.

CHAPTER 2

SPIRITUALITY AS
A BELIEF SYSTEM

'Your treasure house is within; it contains all you'll ever need.'

HUI-HAI

Spirituality is commonly misunderstood. I have always understood spirituality and religion to be two different belief systems.

Spirituality is a belief system, an ideology, a set of principles that help us make sense of our everyday realities.

Often, when people talk about religion, they bring their beliefs about religion into discussions about spirituality. Though religions do emphasise spiritualism as being part of their faith, you can be spiritual without being religious, or a member of an organised religion.

Spirituality is an individual practice and has everything to do with a sense of purpose and peace. It relates to purpose and developing beliefs around life and our connection with others, without any set spiritual values.

Some people may choose to believe in an after-life and follow a moral code of conduct, but do not associate themselves with a particular religion or denomination. However, since it affects the way a person views the world and defines how they treat others, it still counts as a belief system.

THE UNIVERSAL LAWS

I am not sure how old I was when I began to understand the universe and its laws. Whether we believe in them or not, universal laws are there to act, to bring us back into line. It's like an invisible thread, it weaves its magic and works with us, whether we are aware of it or not. It listens, it hears and it acts.

When we convince ourselves we can't do something, the universe conspires to make that happen, in the same way that when we tell ourselves we can do something, the universe also conspires to make that happen. It is not something we can change.

When we begin to understand how the universe works and apply its rules into our everyday lives, our lives can begin to change for the better.

MORAL CODES

We hope our children will follow the moral codes we teach them, but there are no guarantees. It is hard for any parent to stand back, whilst they watch their child live their lives differently.

Morality is often self-taught. It is not something we need an education for, anyone can learn about it. There is no reason why anyone can't think about and use morality for themselves; it just takes practice.

The world is changing and so is morality. There is an art to expression and an art to understanding how to use morality. It has become too easy for people to assume and demand, without giving consideration to the way they ask, and speak to others. We need to continue to keep an open mind, instead of making broad assumptions.

As a child, I innately knew how to behave. When I was growing up, respect and morality was something my generation seemed to grasp diligently. We sponged it up. It was almost expected that we would live our lives with the same values as our parents and grandparents. Morality isn't about education, it is about understanding, a place, an acceptance that we choose to work and live with the standards of right and wrong.

If continually practiced, morality can bring about a sense of calm, a sense of peace and a sense of belonging. As children grow up in today's world, technology often becomes their main focus, as they continue to keep pace with what's going on around them.

If children don't use morality, their peers won't either. Peer pressure may often change how children function and view the world. It is sad, and frustrating for the parents.

ACCOUNTABILITY

Accountability can't be ignored. If we want to create a culture of accountability so we can all live together in harmony, then accountability starts with us.

We need to start by being responsible for ourselves. We need to take ownership of our decisions and when we make commitments, we should meet them. If we ignore being accountable, others will too. We should choose to be accountable.

It isn't something you do once. It's an all-time thing. If one person ignores being accountable, then it can open the floodgates for others to ignore and be selective. That said, the more accountable we are, the more the universe can help us meet with success.

We should stop putting the blame on others and whining about our lives. When we veer off course, it signifies our lack of accountability and responsibility towards our own actions. Instead we should be proactive. We can never succeed in the true sense, without facing our responsibilities and making ourselves accountable. Instead, we should choose to be mindful and keep an open mind.

When we choose not to accept facts, we're telling and showing others we're not accountable, and the universe can never condone that. In the long term without accountability, we will most likely struggle, mentally, emotionally and physically.

For those of us who are accountable, the universe will always want to help us meet with continued success. Life is about accountability. No one escapes it.

EXTENDING OUR VALUES

I believe that sowing a seed with children in their formative years means they will have the opportunities to reap the benefits later on. Of course, there are no guarantees, it is the nature of raising children, but it also very much depends on whether children agree with their parents' values.

My own spiritual values have taught me so much about how I want to live my life, and although I haven't insisted my children share the same values, they know how and what my values mean.

Although we wouldn't want our children to be clones of us, we hope they will evaluate what they've learnt from us, so they get the best out of their relationships and their lives. After all, that is what being a parent is all about.

As parents, we cannot expect the people in our children's lives to conform to their values, but it should be up to our children to decide whether those people are right for them. Whilst having many influences in their lives, we also hope that, as parents, our values continue to resonate with them. As we sow a seed, and our children grow, that they should want to aspire to the same values.

SELFLESSNESS

Being selfless means being focused on the needs of others, rather than our own needs. It is one of the most endearing qualities we can possess.

It is important we are selfless, and we put others first. That doesn't mean we neglect ourselves; we can still do both. People who are selfless are giving. It's within all of our grasps. Being selfless is the spiritual way.

Selfless people are ready to put others first and will express concern for others. Selflessness helps us to expand our thinking and how we perceive our world. We may put people first because we know it's right, because we're generous, and because we're kind.

Selflessness is its own reward. It's a quality that makes people and society better, and communities sweeter. When you are selfless, it is a quality you instinctively identify with, and appreciate and see in others.

People who are selfless continue to think about how their actions may affect others. It means they want to judge less. Selflessness is an important key to relationships, friendships, partnerships and marriage. It helps keep relationships real, keeps individuals grounded and humble.

To be selfless, we need to listen more and practice being kind. We can choose to perform random acts of kindness, giving without expecting back, being patient, and treating others how we would like to be treated.

Selflessness is essential if we are to find contentment and fulfilment in our lives, but it may often be overlooked, because others may sometimes take advantage of those who are.

CONFIRMATION, A SIGN

Every now and again, something or someone may come into our lives, often fleetingly. Usually it is a sign from the universe letting us know that it is aware, that it knows our circumstances and what we're going through. It is a comforting message from the universe to let us know that it understands.

This happened to me while I was watching an episode of Gordon Ramsay's *Kitchen Nightmares* reality show that really hit home; it was as if I were looking at my own life through the eyes of this family, whose Lebanese father had opened up a restaurant: the restaurant was failing, which is why Ramsay had been brought in.

In that moment, I finally understood my life through another person's eyes. We may often have or see a sign, see our lives through another person's; the life they endure is our life, the life they've lived, the life they tried to change, but never could. And as we watch another person's struggle, we may relate to them; their thoughts, their feelings, wanting change, and wishing their lives were different.

I believe it is through these random signs the universe acknowledges our struggles in life, a sign for us that our struggles are understood.

LOSS OF A LOVED ONE

Losing a loved one may often leave us struggling, not always because they've passed, but because of the problems they leave behind that may have affected us.

After losing a loved one, there may be many people left with countless unresolved issues, which can leave them angry, or confused. In life, we may not always be able to change the things that happen to us. We may not always be able to change where we're at with someone before he or she passed; all we can do is find understanding on the life we've had and change how we move forward. It is also pointless holding on to animosity, because it stops us from healing and moving on with our lives.

For many people going through the grieving process, it can take a number of years for them to adjust. Death is part of the living process; it is part of life. It isn't commonly spoken about, but death isn't final. As we come from spirit before our physical lives, we go back to spirit.

Where our loved ones have passed, it is part of a process where they continue to live their lives in spirit, in another form. They are always around us. For many people, letting go is their biggest challenge, and that is part of the grieving process.

SIGNS OF OUR LOVED ONES

If like me you believe in spirit, your spirit guides deliver little signs that your loved ones are trying to communicate with you. Whether something good happens, or you're struggling and just need help, your spirit guides deliver signs that remind you that your loved ones aren't far away. That never diminishes.

While out for a drive shortly after my mum passed, I received signs that showed she wasn't far away. The car driving behind us had part of a number plate that read 'mum'. On returning to our car, the car in front of us also displayed the word 'mum' on the number plate; then as I gazed over to my left, a car also drove past with 'dad' written on that number plate.

There are also other signs. Lights flickering and feathers that seem to appear from nowhere. The whole spiritual thing can send shivers down the spine for those who are slightly spooked by the idea, but for me, the messages they leave are tokens of love to say that our loved ones are still around us, that all is good with them.

For those who choose not to believe, they may be a sceptic. Anyone who is unwilling to open their mind to the possibility that loved ones are trying to connect, may be less open-minded in other areas of their lives too. It is all about keeping an open mind.

Knowing both my parents agreed and did so at the same time was slightly weird for me, particularly as they weren't always in sync with each other on this side of life.

BENEFITS OF SELFLESSNESS

There are benefits to being selfless. Being able to do anything selflessly, means you're helping to expand your sense of self, the sense of who you are. It means you're less vanity focused, less jealous and consequently less mean.

When we act selfishly, we are limited to a thinking that only benefits ourselves. Where selfish acts hinder emotional and spiritual growth, selfless acts build on emotional and spiritual growth.

Being selfless means you're not acting on your ego, or that you have a desire to prove yourself to others. In a world that is constantly changing, we should be selfless. Selflessness means you're working without the ego; it means you want to help others.

If you give help to others, you should want to do it selflessly, not anticipate or expect a reward back. If you give help to others, and you expect recognition returned, consciously or unconsciously, this is not selflessness.

The benefits of selflessness mean you're in tune with your higher self and the universe. It also means you're identifying with others and you're choosing to make a difference.

TRUST AND TRUTH

As a young child, I didn't know what trust or truth was, but I don't think you do when you're young. I didn't stop to question either, but I would rather have been told something I didn't want to hear, than have ignored what I needed to hear.

Truth and trust should start with family. As adults, it is important we live with trust and truth in place, we need both for mental and emotional stability; it is important we can trust and hear the truth. We need to be able to trust others to tell us the truth.

It is important we tell the truth no matter how difficult it is. On our part, we may be afraid to say something, to tell the truth for fear of causing offence. Indeed, some may expect us to agree with their opinions, and take offence when what we say doesn't tie in with their beliefs.

We shouldn't have to say something they want to hear; they should trust us to speak the truth, as we should trust them. Simply put, without truth there is no trust and without trust, there can be no truth.

JUDGMENT AND SPIRITUALITY

We all have a soul and every soul has a spirit. It is important for the soul to have spiritual awareness, knowledge and insight. Who we are today is not who we will be tomorrow, or who we were yesterday. As individuals we grow, and we evolve.

I have never tried to make anyone believe what I believe, or judged someone for what they believe. It is simply not my way.

Spirituality paves the way for us to understand how life works and what our lessons are. For those who judge, they do so because they are less aware of their values and spiritual path.

We may spend a lifetime forming judgments. But where our beliefs are an interpretation of our experiences, they may never be right for anyone else. Judgments are based on beliefs and beliefs are based on individual perceptions.

Because we all see our experiences differently, it would be wrong for us to act as judge and jury on other people's opinions. If through a conversation someone is happy to believe what we're telling them, then our beliefs and judgments can be accepted.

It is not for us to try to convert anyone else to believe what we believe, or for anyone else to convert, or judge us back.

MISUNDERSTANDING KARMA

Karma is one of the most misunderstood Buddhist teachings. We often think that karma is some kind of external force that punishes us for our bad deeds and rewards us for our good. But it is not external, nor is it about punishments, or rewards. Karma means action. It refers to the intentions behind an action, broadly explained as anything we might say or do.

Intentions may be seen as skilful or unskilful. Skilful is where our intentions encompass qualities of clarity, mindfulness, contentment and care for the well-being of others and ourselves. Unskilful is where our intentions are motivated by selfishness, impulse, greed, confusion and ill will.

When we act without selfish intent, with clarity and mindfulness, our actions lead to an increase in ease, peace and happiness. However we choose to act, we alone choose the consequences of those actions. It has nothing to do with an external force. In short, we can create our happiness and suffering through our own actions.

As the Buddha said, 'What a man wills, what he plans, what he dwells on, forms the basis for the continuation of consciousness.' Basically, we are masters of our own destiny.

We create our consciousness through our thoughts and actions, and in doing so, not only do we create our actions, but our actions create us. Mindfulness can free us from this loop, by breaking the cycle and changing it into a path that leads to awakening.

This mindfulness is necessary, because without it, we may become engrossed deep in our thoughts and feelings, which means we may struggle to stand back; struggle to be reflective, which in turn may strengthen our unenlightened habits.

We need to realise that if we act in one way, for example angrily, then there will be consequences. On the other hand, if we act with patience and kindness, then the consequences should be more beneficial. It is not enough just to know what we should do; we also have to act.

Karma is essentially our own self-balancing mechanism, or feedback that shows us the extent to which we're in tune with our reality.

PRINCIPLES OF MORALITY

If you believe in karma, you will know we are not punished for our sins, but by them. If we abuse for long enough, the very things that are precious to us will be the very things we lose.

In everyday life, we do it to ourselves and don't stop to think. We cannot make decisions based on our own self-absorbed thinking, and still expect our lives to work out. We are judged on our intent. If we choose to put someone in a position just so we can better ourselves, then we can expect karma back.

Karma always come back worse than what we hand out. By association, innocent people who have dealings with us, can also get caught up in the crossfire and that's not fair. Karma isn't something we experience individually either.

'Dangerous consequences will follow when politicians and rulers forget moral principles. Whether we believe in God or karma, ethics is the founder of every religion' – Dalai Lama. In other words, when the people whose job it is to protect and look after the people they serve lose their morality, terrible things can occur. Everything bad that is happening in the world is happening as a consequence.

It is important world leaders, and society as a whole, do

more to correct their behaviour and immorality, so we can all heal.

THE WOUNDED PSYCHE

I want to elaborate and explain a little more about the psyche, because it is very much the catalyst for our behaviour traits.

The psyche has two parts. The part that we don't want to see or feel is called the 'shadow' and the part that we accept is called the 'persona'. The shadow is the bad or dark side of our personality.

In reality, neither the shadow nor the persona are an accurate representation of who we are deep down. They are both exaggerations and distortions of us, as each only conveys a part. The shadow includes early childhood experiences that we may not have dealt with that were too traumatic for us to consciously process.

The persona is the part of us we're comfortable with, that we allow others to see. The parts we're not comfortable with, we tend to hide. Over a period of time, we may develop our persona in order to win the acceptance and approval of others. The persona is a mask we wear, in an attempt to hide what we feel.

We tend to think that if we hide what we feel, then we won't have to deal with those feelings. But the mask we sometimes wear may tell a different story. Wearing the mask is an attempt to hide what we really feel inside. It can be hard to understand the person behind their mask, unless they remove it.

It may be a matter of time before the mask wears thin, and the person behind the mask reveals his or her true self, how they are through a damaged psyche. When the psyche is damaged, we may begin to emotionally struggle.

Not all people are broken, but for those who see themselves as broken, it doesn't just happen overnight. Being broken starts with the past, with our experiences. Once we are able to understand our past and deal with and put our experiences behind us, the psyche can have a chance to heal.

When we can move on from our past comfortably, the psyche can heal and return to completeness, and we can get a realistic sense of who we are.

PURPOSEFUL CONNECTIONS

It is fascinating when we begin to understand how the universe connects with us and how those connections bring people into our lives, if only for a brief moment. On our part, it is important we understand why people aren't supposed to stay, or why we're not supposed to stay in other people's lives.

Often, people may come into our lives fleetingly, with a message that helps us to move on. They may come at a time when we're either mentally or emotionally stuck, but initially, we may not always be aware of how those connections work. Unless you follow the spiritual path, you won't consciously stop to think about these ephemeral connections, why they happen or what they mean, but others, who practice and understand how spirit timing works, should be completely aware.

Purposeful connections are there specifically to help us look at our lives, to bring what we're doing into focus, so that we can work through those things and choose to do them differently. They are usually there for a purpose. But the connection is often fleeting; the universe doesn't advertise, so it would be easy for us to miss its connection and message.

With all purposeful connections we need to continue to be consciously aware, so we don't miss the signs or their meaning, and to read between the lines. Comments or conversations meant for us will always reach us, usually appearing in the form of a message. But like Morse code, we need to be adept at recognising its signs.

Loved ones who have passed, may also come into our lives at certain points, because the universe believes we need their help at that time, and we need to accept their messages are exactly what we need. We should also accept the universe believes we are ready to accept those messages, so that we may learn from them.

The universe intervenes if it knows what we're doing isn't selfless, or that what we're doing isn't getting us the right response, or result. The universe imparts the information we need so that we can help ourselves work through any new approach.

We mustn't become complacent or continue to lead blindly. It is also not enough for us to just live. We need to understand our lives, why we're here, and why we have purposeful connections.

We need to try to open our eyes, to understand those brief connections, so we may interpret and decipher the information we are being given. Often, it is simply because what we're doing isn't right, and we need to reassess.

OUR CONSCIENCE

A conscience is the inner sense of an individual, of what is right or wrong in one's conduct or motives. For those who don't think about, live, or work with their conscience, they may work under the guise that a conscience is for others.

The conscience is part of the cognitive process that elicits rational associations and emotions, based on doing what's right in a community, in society and with family.

Working with our conscience allows us to think about what is right and wrong and do what is right, no matter what. From a moral standpoint, we should all be using our conscience, so that we are continually doing right by others. The conscience should be used to help us form responsible judgments.

The conscience is a reality check on decisions made and yet to make. It epitomises moral action. It is the inner sense of our conduct and motives, requiring us to do the right thing and pointing us in the direction it wants us to go.

ENVIRONMENTAL CONSCIOUSNESS

It's important to consciously think about our planet and the 'universe' as we go about our daily lives, think about global warming and how we're contributing to problems with the planet. We should want to do more.

We need to be mindful too, consciously think about things as we're doing them. For example, do you remember to switch your outside house light off before you go to bed? Do you remember to turn the light off when you're leaving a room? Do you really need to wash a single item in the washing machine?

It may be just a simple mental block, but to help us save the planet, it is something we should all remember to do. In the same token, we need to be more environmentally friendly. We should use less paper and recycle more; make sure we're using the right light bulbs; choose cloth over paper; use canvas bags instead of using plastic; eat less meat; use a compost bin for food waste; reduce water waste; live a greener life and do without one more luxury.

These things affect us all, and they affect our planet. They are things we should all think about and focus on, to help ease the pressure on the planet, and to safeguard our children and their children's futures. While many of us are aware of the need to be responsible about these issues, we should collectively think about being more selfless.

LEARNING TO INTROSPECT

We know that introversion, or introspection is the act of observing and thinking about ourselves and our lives objectively. Introspection is a conversation within us. Both are used as a tool to help us look at our lives from the outside in.

With introspection you look at how you talk, what you say and how you behave, how you feel and what makes you feel the way you feel. Through introspection you come to understand yourself, and your experiences. Introspection helps you look at and question certain aspects of your life, so that you can manage any issues you're struggling to deal with.

Through introspection, you find elements of your parents, similarities and disagreements with your siblings, anyone you have shared an experience with. You also find certain influences around your experiences, issues with experiences that include dysfunctional behaviour, such as neglect, abuse and trauma.

If introversion or introspection is done properly, you come away with a more balanced and fair opinion of your experiences; you also see and understand everyone's part in your lives, so that you're looking at the bigger picture.

Introspection is not about apportioning blame, or finding fault with others. Finding fault simply adds fuel to an already burning fire. Introspection simply gives a balanced and fair account of your experiences so that you are able to move on.

Introspection is about understanding and coming to terms with your experiences. It helps you find peace.

BEING MINDFUL OF YOUR ACTIONS

Being mindful isn't just about being alerted to something and then being mindful of your actions. It is about paying attention to your environment, and living in the present.

It is also not something we all have in our lifetime; that part is up to us. Being mindful is something we should practice and something that can have a positive impact on both our personal and professional life.

Being mindful helps us improve ourselves and our relationships. It is listening carefully to what others have to say, looking at our lifestyles, trying meditation and incorporating that into our daily routine.

It is important to practice being mindful. For example, focus on your breathing, use visualisation, think about and be aware of your feelings. Analyse your thoughts. Think about how you feel, and why you feel how you do. Think about your experiences. It is not just your experience in that moment that makes you feel unhappy, or angry.

Being mindful is something that we can all benefit from, for us to work successfully together, for us to make the world a more secure place. It's something we can teach ourselves. We should train our mind to see the good in people, in society and in the world, so that we can change our internal dialogue, so that we can use empathy, compassion and tolerance, instead of irritability, anger and abuse.

We should never assume something without really knowing, or understanding. It is important we change our lifestyle, so we can become more mindful and acknowledge our progress. The more mindful we are, the more benefits we bring to our lives and to those around us.

USING REFLECTION AS A TOOL

Through reflection, we learn that although the past cannot be changed, those times are when we learn our most precious lessons: that no matter how difficult the past is, it is important we find a way through.

Reflection teaches us that just because someone is silent, doesn't mean they have nothing to say. That kindness, compassion, tolerance and empathy towards ourselves and others needs to be honed and continue to be honed, that we can spiritually and mentally grow through our experiences.

We may also learn that no response is a powerful response, and that sometimes it is the only response needed. We don't have to have the last word for us to feel empowered, that courage is coming through fear and is about not giving up.

Through reflection, we can learn a lot about ourselves, and that we can only change ourselves. We also learn about others who were, or are still part of our life.

A PATH TO ENLIGHTENMENT

The path that leads to enlightenment is the path we take to better ourselves; better our lives, become better people and become more spiritually aware.

But in order to attain spiritual awareness, we have to be in touch with the truth and continually work on it. Enlightenment isn't something that just happens, it is something we may continue to develop.

The foundation that helps us achieve enlightenment is progress. Progress means we are making headway, but our starting point should be self-awareness. Also, we should be more tolerant and patient, less opinionated and judgmental and more empathetic towards others and what they may be dealing with.

Enlightenment is having a wider understanding of our responsibilities in the world and our place in it; being able to grow and be a positive influence on others, and in the world. Having harmony as part of that process allows us to improve ourselves, without hurting others and spreading happiness to people.

The path to enlightenment is not an easy path, but it is one that if practiced regularly can continue to give us the most peace in our lives, and with each other.

HOW THE UNIVERSE WORKS

The universe is instrumental in all our lives, but it's

something we need to understand if we are to have access to it and use it successfully.

We may observe its teachings, but in order to have access, we need to first explore what goes on inside our mind. Failing to do so means our truths, how we want our lives to be, may remain at a distance.

I could never have imagined, as a child, the success I would gain through the diagnosis of my disability, but the universe had other ideas. It had already carved out my life, waiting for me to mentally, emotionally and to spiritually catch up.

So, how does the universe work? Access to the universe starts with our thoughts. What we intend is what we will create. We need to train our minds to consciously choose our thoughts, so the thoughts we focus on show up more in our lives. If we continually focus positively on our challenges, we should have an abundance of challenges that become positive.

When we continually think about things in abundance and with a greater passion, the more we can create in that area. Abundance is attracted to us, based on how we feel; so the more positive our thoughts, the more positive the outcome. It is not always our circumstances, rather our thoughts that change what happens; but it is our attitude that may let us down. We have the power to choose.

From an early age, unconsciously I had already decided I wasn't giving up. I never gave up hope, my thoughts remained steadfast throughout my childhood.

When we think a certain way, we begin to feel a certain way. Focus your thoughts on what *is*, and you will create more of the same. Choose to focus your thoughts on what could *be*, and you open your mind and heart to amazing possibilities.

So, instead of spending more time choosing what you want to buy or wear, think about the people you connect with and how they feel. All it takes is one positive thought to create a string of continuous positive thoughts and that in turn creates opportunities.

THE UNIVERSE SPEAKS

Whether we believe in the universe and its laws is immaterial to the universe. It will always catch up with us on the things we ignore. Even if we don't understand how it works, or we ignore its signs, the universe will send out a sign for us to pick up on. The universe speaks, but we're sometimes blissfully unaware.

Signs may come in the form of an instinct; a sense of inner knowing that something is true, even though it feels implausible. The sign may also be an answer that directs us down a certain path we probably wouldn't have taken, or even considered.

If something seems much harder than it should be, it's usually a sign from the universe that what we're trying to do isn't working, and that perhaps we should think about taking a different path.

The universe will also catch up with us on the things that it deems improper and may serve to right that wrong.

No one is exempt; when we learn to listen to the universe, our lives become more effortless.

OUR JOURNEY'S PURPOSE

There is a spiritual belief that trauma, and the difficulties around traumatic experiences, are the symptoms of having lost sight of the purpose of our journey.

But perhaps it is not always those who have experienced trauma that have lost sight, but those who inflict trauma on others, who have lost sight of their own purpose. I didn't lose sight of my journey; what I had to deal with became the purpose of my journey.

Where we're not always able to change things, it is the daily practice of gratitude for life's journey that is available to each of us, which pulls us through.

THE KNOWING UNIVERSE

The universe knows us more than we know ourselves. Although consciously I never gave the universe a thought as a child, innately I always felt there was something bigger than myself.

Now when I look back, I see that my experiences have shaped and defined my life. My blog wouldn't exist without it. All possibilities happen through 'divine timing', the idea that everything happens at its exact right time.

The universe doesn't work to a pre-set list of wants, because life is about what we need, not what we want. We should continually be open to the universe. We limit our possibilities if we are determined to ask for what we think we want.

The universe is happy to oblige, but we should never try to control the outcome. Having a little faith, and accepting that things happen for a reason, helps us understand why things happen the way they do, but we should always apply our thinking and look for our lessons.

We should also look at the bigger picture; look at things from a broader perspective, because that should give us more clarity, more understanding and a better vantage point for us to understand why things happen the way they do.

Being wrong about what we think we want or need is the best way to learn. We struggle in the present, so that we may learn how not to struggle in the future. What we think we need isn't the same as what is possible.

Things only happen when they are supposed to. I believe it is important we put our trust in the universe, that we get what we're supposed to get at the right 'divine time'.

THE UNIVERSE CONSPIRES

When we do things for our own gain because we're greedy, or we think we're entitled, the universe has its own ideas on whether it feels we deserve it. When we look back with the benefit of hindsight, it is easy to see how we handled ourselves and whether we could have handled ourselves differently.

There may be times when we look back and see how we should have handled ourselves because the outcome wasn't what we intended, or wanted.

When we behave in ways that get the best out of others, we hope they will want to reciprocate. We are also asking the universe to accept we are behaving well and, in doing so, asking that what we're trying to do will work out for us.

SPIRITUAL AWARENESS

I don't know how old I was when I became aware of a built-in intuition that became my 'eyes and ears' and 'spiritual awareness'. When I was angry, it never presented itself, but in my more lucid moments, it was there. The older I got and the more I understood my experiences, the more I was able to control my anger, then only every now and again would that part of me be seen.

Spiritual growth is a process of inner awakening, where we start to become aware of our 'inner-self'. Being aware of our inner-self helps us to develop a higher awareness, so that we're able to tap into our unconscious thinking: it enables us to go beyond what is in our conscious thoughts, to help us bring understanding of who we are, what makes us, us now and in past experiences. We all have this ability, but usually that part of who we are is tucked away behind the ego personality.

The ego personality is the combination of the perception

we have of ourselves and the values that we attribute to our experiences in our past, which may often lead to us evaluating ourselves more highly than we should.

Instead, being spiritual allows us to instinctively listen to our inner thoughts, so that we are continually tuned in. Having spiritual beliefs helps us become better, more compassionate people.

Spiritual beliefs also allow us to live a more peaceful and tranquil life. They help us take away fear, anxiety and stress; they also help us to compose ourselves so that we are able to remain calm under pressure with whatever we have to deal with.

THE LAWS OF THE UNIVERSE

The universe is different to religion or science, neither of which have the answers about the way it works. The universe operates in accordance with laws. Some of these laws are physical and some are spiritual. An example of a physical law you might be familiar with is the law of gravity. But we may also take part in spiritual laws, such as the law of reciprocity, which means that when you give your time and energy selflessly to help others, those things come back to you.

To function successfully and harmoniously and with each other, we need to learn to abide by the universal laws and work together.

The universe works on the metaphysical laws below:

THE LAW OF DIVINE ONENESS

The first law is the law that explains how each of us are part of one universal energy. This is why hating someone, or wishing them harm is harmful. When we do this, we are in effect hating, or wishing harm on ourselves.

THE LAW OF VIBRATION

All things are made of energy and the law of vibration states that we need to align our energy with what we want to attract. We should express our emotions in healthy ways and focus on emotions, such as love and gratitude, as much as we can. This helps us to attract higher things back into our lives.

THE LAW OF ACTION

We are human, but we are also divine. We should embrace our experience here on earth, in order to grow and learn the lessons of our current journey. This doesn't mean pain, hard work and struggle. Challenges help us to learn and grow. However, if we find ourselves constantly struggling, we may need to reconnect with our higher selves.

This helps us to discover the lifestyle and goals that help us grow without struggle.

THE LAW OF CORRESPONDENCE

This universal law states that, like a mirror, your outer world reflects your inner world. The world outside mirrors our inner self. What we choose to focus on becomes our reality, whether it is good or bad.

THE LAW OF CAUSE AND EFFECT

This law states that what you reap you will sow. Many spiritual traditions have taught this universal wisdom for thousands of years. The most well-known of which is the Law of Karma.

If we harm others, we are ultimately harming ourselves. However, if we work for the highest good, of ourselves and others, and from motives of love and compassion, we find this reflected in the people and events that occur in our lives.

THE LAW OF COMPENSATION

Instead of wishing things were different, we have to be different. Whatever we feel is lacking in our lives is probably something that we aren't giving. Whether it is money, time, recognition or love, practice giving it to yourself and others first. This can change your energy and your world.

THE LAW OF PERPETUAL TRANSMUTATION OF ENERGY

This last spiritual law is about how we react to the world around us. We sometimes think that the only way to change our world is to try harder, or struggle. We worry about what might happen to us, and we try to control things in order to feel better. When we do this, we restrict energy flow.

If we let go of control over life and learn to go with the flow a little more, our energy can start moving again. We need to have faith in the universal laws, the universe and ourselves. Whatever happens, we need to understand that we have the inner resources to deal with things.

It is important we work with the universe and its laws. For the universe to work with us, we should operate on at least these four laws: action, consequence, positive energy and the power of choice. Once we do that, we may find over time the universe will want to start responding and working with us, so making our lives easier.

Whilst we continue to work against the universe and what we want for ourselves, the universe may stop working with us, and each other. This can have a knock-on effect upon our lives, our children's lives, in society and communities as a whole, and as a result we may struggle to find the right path and/or success. (Source: https://www.learning-mind.com)

MESSAGES FROM THE UNIVERSE

The universe teaches us that no matter how difficult life gets, we should speak our truth because it is the right thing to do. We cannot pre-empt, anticipate, or know how others will behave, but that is for them to reconcile.

If someone's behaviour is the reason why things don't work out for us, then that adds to their karma, not ours. By doing what is right, even if the other person doesn't, we absolve ourselves of any responsibility.

The universe is always aware of our circumstances and may continue to send us messages; but we need to be ready to recognise its signs so that we can receive its messages. Where our initial circumstances may have changed, the universe tries to create new circumstances to help us right any potential wrong.

Regardless of whether we redress the balance or get to the final outcome, it is important we make ourselves emotionally stronger through the process, so that we are able to move into a better mental and emotional space. Doing so means we can then start to make better decisions for ourselves, and for others too. We may also get to see and understand the bigger picture, and for us to communicate what we need from others to help us.

The universe will continually invite us to seek out answers, to understand why our lives turn out a certain way and what we can personally do to change how things turn out. Once we apply the laws, we automatically take charge and redirect, continuing to shape our lives in the way we want our lives to go.

The more we apply the universal laws, the more we can intuitively and spiritually grow. When we intuitively and spiritually grow, we consciously become aware of everything and everyone around us and that's when we can gain more control of our lives.

Our lives then become more meaningful, we are more at peace with ourselves and that reflects in our attitude, in our behaviour and in our relationships.

CHAPTER 3

NURTURING A SPIRITUAL LIFE

'Your sacred space is where you can find yourself over and over again.'

JOSEPH CAMPBELL

Nurturing a spiritual life is allowing the universe to help you accomplish things and surrendering and trusting in it, even when you cannot foresee the outcome. But first, you should nurture the concept of how the universe works, and also understand how spirit and divine timing works.

'Divine timing' means everything unfolds perfectly, when it's supposed to. It is important we don't force situations, rather wait for things to happen at the exact time; know things happen for a reason and that timing is everything.

We are all spiritual beings. It is important we nurture our understanding of what is a spiritual life. When we listen to our intuition and surrender to spirit, we lessen our struggles. We free ourselves from doubt and fear, releasing obstacles through our deeper understanding and awareness of how everything in the universe works.

OUR MORAL COMPASS

A moral compass is a person's ability to judge what is right and wrong and act accordingly. It is partly responsible for the way we live our lives; the other part is our values.

But we need to understand how a moral compass works, for us to incorporate moral values into our lives. We need to also understand our experiences, work with our moral compass, and use our values as a guide.

Without the use of a moral compass, we may struggle to get the best out of life. A moral compass dictates our ability to make the right judgments around our decisions and judgments towards other people.

LOOKING AFTER NATURE

Bringing nature into our everyday lives will help us value it, encouraging us to incorporate more sustainable behaviours, as well as connect with ourselves and each other.

Valuing nature is desperately needed. Nature is struggling to survive and needs our help. Nature and the human species share the same ecosystem; therefore, it is important we look after nature and start to experience all that it has to offer.

We need to value nature, so that it looks after us. Being outdoors has other rewards too. Being surrounded by it is good for our mental, emotional and spiritual health. In light of what is going on in the world, making a connection with the natural world has never been so important.

Nature not only helps us connect with and appreciate wildlife, but it also helps us connect with ourselves, sometimes in solitude, sometimes not, but always connecting us with it.

As David Attenborough concludes in his *Extinction* documentary, the human species and nature need to coexist together, if nature and the human species are to survive.

Spending time outdoors is good for us. People who do so tend to be happier, healthier and more relaxed about their lives. Connecting with nature helps us think about our life in the whole; it helps us to identify with ourselves and with our lives, which means we're more likely to want to change our outward behaviour.

Looking after the natural world has never been so important. No matter the weather, bask in all its glory; get yourself wrapped up and get out there.

BENEFITS OF PATIENCE

Patience is essential to daily life and is the key to us having a happy, more tranquil existence. Having patience means being able to wait, or deal with a situation calmly, and is something we should take time to practice.

There are many benefits of patience. Patient people experience less depression, cope better in stressful situations, and also experience fewer negative emotions. They are more mindful; they have more gratitude and a greater sense of abundance.

Patient people have better mental health. They feel less agitated by things than those people who struggle to wait. People who are more patient are also more hopeful and more satisfied with their lives.

Patience is something learned. If your parents are patient, you will more likely be patient, but even if they're not, it is something you can learn. Patient people have more time for others, they are selfless, agreeable and kind. They are flexible and more likely to trust.

They are tolerant, likely to be more generous and show more compassion. Patient people are also more likely to forgive. Patience gives us sticking power, meaning we're less likely to give up; therefore we're more likely to also achieve our goals.

Patient people are less likely to jump from job to job. They're also more likely to have reduced stress. Patience can protect against damage to our health.

RECOGNISING FAULT

Do we recognise our faults? There's something about the human condition that makes us hesitant to admit when we're at fault. Even when it becomes obvious to everyone else, we may still not be prepared to admit we are wrong.

Some of us can go through life never admitting our faults, or recognising when we're wrong, but may still be quick off the mark to recognise, or point out other people's faults. We may not always understand, or recognise our behaviour traits because we're not aware what they are.

When we are able to recognise our issues and address them, we are more likely to admit we were at fault and change our presenting behaviour.

MORALITY AND EDUCATION

Although schools aim to raise awareness of the importance of self-worth, and how we behave in our relationships, this is not done in a wider spiritual context. Primary and secondary school students should be stimulated to question their sense of wonder in the world and how as individuals they belong in it. There are questions children should be encouraged to ask such as:

- What is the meaning and purpose to life?
- What values do I have?
- What makes me truly happy?
- What happens to me when I die?

These questions bring about a spiritual awareness, of the importance of respect for ourselves and our planet. Empathy, compassion and tolerance can positively influence learning and well-being.

Children should be made aware of their moral compass, they should be taught morality through spirituality by their parents or care givers, in a wider spiritual context, and then it should be reinforced through education.

Morality is crucial and necessary in everyday life. It matters because it means we live our daily lives while being concerned about key moral values, such as honesty and respect, equality, fairness and justice, compassion and right and wrong.

NATURE V NURTURE

Nature means the genetic and hereditary factors that influence who we are, from our physical appearance to our personalities; whereas nurture refers to environmental factors that have an impact on who we are, including our early childhood experiences, how we are raised, our social relationships and our surrounding culture.

The nature versus nurture debate is one of the oldest debated topics in psychology. Different branches of psychology have tended to take a one versus the other approach. The longstanding debate centres around the relative contributions of genetic inheritance and environmental factors to human development, to which there are many different approaches.

Some philosophers such as Plato suggest that certain

things are natural, or they occur naturally, regardless of environmental influences. Other well-known philosophers, such as John Locke, suggest that the mind begins as a blank page so that everything that we are, and all of our knowledge, is determined by our experiences.

Empiricists take the view that all, or most behaviours and characteristics result from learning. These behaviourists believe that all actions and behaviours are the results of conditioning. Some theorists believe that people can be trained to do and become anything, regardless of their genetic background. (Source: https://www.verywellmind.com)

A simple question can raise these issues. For example, when a person excels academically, do they excel because they are genetically predisposed to high intelligence, or is it a result of an enriched environment? When someone has a violent temper, is it because they are born with that tendency, or is it something learned by observing another person's behaviour?

Some characteristics are tied to environmental influences. How a person behaves can be linked to influences such as parenting styles and learned experiences. For example, a child might learn through observation and reinforcement to say 'please' and 'thank you'. Another child might learn to behave aggressively by observing older children engaging in violent behaviour in the playground.

Throughout the history of psychology, this debate has continued to stir up controversy, although today, the majority of experts believe that *both* nature and nurture influence behaviour and development.

Increasingly, people are beginning to see that asking how much heredity or environment influence a particular trait isn't the right approach. There isn't a simple way to unscramble the influences that exist.

Although genetics and environment play their part, we can still learn things like empathy, compassion, tolerance and patience. There is always room for improvement, room to change if we want to change, lives are not set in stone. We should consciously think about what we want to get out of our lives.

We shouldn't rely on our parentage or childhood conditioning to see us through, we should rely on our own thinking.

STAY HUMBLE

In a world where we're encouraged to be anything but humble, choose to be humble. Being humble in a world that is fast changing makes you stand apart from the rest.

Feel a sense of humility and judge no one. In a world where you're expected to prove yourself, the only test is to yourself. When we place two feet firmly on the ground, we become grounded in that moment. Being humble keeps us grounded. When we're humble, and we have two feet firmly on the ground we have a sense of 'knowing'.

When we are grounded, we don't need to shout about our accomplishments, because knowing where we stand as a human being is more important. The universe isn't interested and doesn't expect us to measure how great we are against how great someone else is. That's not why we're here: understanding why we're here sets the tone for life.

And with humility, keeping both feet firmly on the ground gives us peace. Being humble gives us a different perspective and understanding of how we should be living our lives. Being humble means we're happy to place less importance on ourselves; to know that not everything has to be about us helps take the stress out of daily life.

We need to let humility act as our guide and our accomplishments, and let us give back to others who need the help more than we do.

RESPECT OTHERS

Although respect is an overall evaluation we give to others, we should actively choose to be respectful. We don't have to agree all the time, but it is important we are respectful.

We are all different and unique. Most of us will have a moral compass guided by our own values, but that doesn't mean others will be guided by our values. Although respect is not a given, it's not for us to comment or pass an opinion, unless someone has done something to us, and we have reason to. Ultimately, respect has to be earned.

For whatever reason we may withhold respect for others, it infers they are not worthy of our respect and that may trigger a decline in those relationships and bring about a negative response. Although this is sometimes necessary for all sorts of legitimate reasons, once we start to believe someone is unworthy of respect, we may potentially open the floodgates to disagreement and argument.

But respect is important, because it's the glue that holds family, friendships, and society together. Having and receiving respect helps us to express ourselves responsibly and appropriately, and fundamentally makes us feel secure.

However, when we follow the universal rules of the road and others don't, it is important we still show respect. It is important we understand their actions are a conversation with the universe, and nothing to do with us.

Individuals are accountable to themselves and the universe. Respecting each other is the universal way.

SELF-WORTH AND OTHERS

Although some of us may have emotional wounds inflicted upon us by others and, as a result, have a lack of self-worth, we owe it to ourselves to make sure we work on healing ourselves.

Emotional wounds can mean bouts of self-pity, as we live with the effects of events that, retrospectively, we couldn't do anything about, although that's not what we may tell ourselves. But it shouldn't be an excuse to stop working on ourselves, or our self-worth. When pity starts to become our main focus, then we know it is time to re-shift our attentions.

We may also experience feelings of self-pity through a

change in circumstances. There are circumstances where self-pity can help us, when it becomes a self-soothing coping mechanism that assists us in accepting and changing our circumstances.

But continually focusing on self-pity for too long can hamper our progress. It can also be self-destructive if through self-pity, and feeling sorry for ourselves, we reach rock bottom. Introspection can always help with this.

MEDIATION AND PROBLEM SOLVING

The way we problem solve may affect the way we behave. Through mediation, we can learn to talk things through, and problem solve. If we understood and used mediation, we might avoid blame.

When it comes to relationships, it is important we mediate. It is even more important for parents to show their children how to mediate, so as their children get older they can use mediation to get the best out of their own relationships.

Parents who manage their problems constructively help protect their children from conflict. When families work together to find solutions, they can form healthier, happier and stronger relationships. A problem-solving approach can help children learn to confront their own worries.

It is important we listen and come from a place of care, rather than a place of blame, so that others don't become the scapegoat. Always focus on the issue and not the person.

EMOTIONALLY BALANCED

We don't often think about whether we are emotionally stable, unless we're struggling and we seek help, but without it, we may begin to mentally struggle. Being emotionally balanced and being 'emotionally stable' is something we all need to strive for.

Emotional stability can help us stay emotionally balanced, and can help us stay grounded so that we don't panic when things go awry. The other side of emotional stability is resilience, both are needed to help us withstand hardships. Having emotional stability helps us to keep our cool under stress.

It helps us weigh up the pros and cons without getting knocked back. Our initial emotional response to how we see negativity is more negative than it probably needs to be. A different perspective is what is needed here.

Like karma checks and balances, so does life. When we choose to look at our issues and circumstances intuitively, in a way that creates positivity, we should find our answers. We innately have the tools to work things out for ourselves, but we should learn to apply those tools to everyday issues and situations.

And when we think we can't, with those acquired tools we can and often do surprise ourselves. That even through issues there are possibilities, a way through; it is important we think about those possibilities and not just look at them. Issues carry lessons, things are not always black and white.

When we learn to look for the positives through the

negatives, from another 'perspective' or our 'intuition', we're looking at our experiences through a different lens. That should then provide a more positive understanding of our lessons and our experiences, and that can bring about emotional stability.

INSIDE AND OUT

We hide our emotions, we bury our vulnerability, we spend our time convincing ourselves we're okay, when inwardly we're not feeling it.

It would be good if taking care of ourselves was just about taking care of our physical well-being. It isn't, because taking care of ourselves means dealing with our emotions. Without keeping our emotions intact, we may struggle with our physical health, and although we may often get by, just getting by means we're not living to our full potential.

But we all have the ability to change. We have the ability to think and understand, to look at our past and to change the way we see and do things, so that we can take good care of ourselves on the inside and out.

A few helpful tips:

- Get to know yourself
- Acknowledge and recognise how you feel
- Look at your life to see where and how you can make changes

- If you're dealing with issues, write down some of them, past and present, so that you recognise how you feel
- Remember that sometimes how you feel is not attributed to you, or your current situation
- If you're still not coping, make an appointment to go and talk to someone
- Distance yourself from those who continue to cause you stress
- If you're not feeling up to it, say no to any commitments you would normally say yes to
- Learn to connect with your inner thoughts so that you're connecting with yourself
- Change your lifestyle to incorporate all the above

When we are able to take better care of our emotional health, we become less vulnerable, we stay well for longer, and we can have more peace.

THE MODERN WORLD

The world I grew up in isn't the world my children have grown up in. In a way, it's not altogether bad that we live in a technologically advanced world, but it's not an altogether good thing either, because it has affected the way children interact with others.

Although improvements in technology have become the catalyst for communication, there are many other factors that need to be taken into consideration. With peer pressure and other outside influences, parents may struggle to understand how they can tap into their children's lives, without having to compete with mobile phones, tablets and games consoles. They may also wonder how they can help to bring about less challenging emotional outcomes for their children in today's modern world.

Technology has the ability to cause more stress, but with so many outside influences and challenges, it's not surprising children rely on, and use technology as a retreat. With technology at their fingertips, they have learned a different way to communicate with their family and friends. Although some children's values are based on their parents' values, those values may not always tie in with how their children choose to live their lives.

Growing up, my values centred on people, not things. We didn't have technology in the same way. We amused ourselves and, in doing so, our lives were simple, less stressful.

Today, communication has become even more important due to the lockdowns and restrictions on movement introduced in 2020 to help limit the spread of Covid-19. It has made us increasingly reliant on technology to keep in touch, both for work and social reasons. Children are communicating more and more through smartphones and tablets, and rely on social media sites to communicate.

Keeping in touch in difficult times is important for our mental health, so we do not feel isolated or alone, and that has to be a good thing.

WHY REFLECTION IS IMPORTANT

Using reflection and looking back on my experiences, I see a very different version of me, the angry child is no longer staring back at me.

Without reflection, I could never have moved on with my life, to achieve what I have. Reflection allows for emotional and spiritual growth. It is important we are able to reflect, recall and find solutions to our problems. It would be difficult to progress without it.

Using reflection helps us identify the parts of us that we need to change. Without it we are less likely to make any changes and changes are necessary if we are to heal, adapt and move forward in our lives.

Don't be afraid to explore your experiences. Give yourself time to work through those. It is easy for us to gloss over our experiences, easy for us to reinvent history, play down the bad times, and put people on a pedestal who don't deserve to be there. It is easy for us to continue to blame ourselves.

Instead, it's important you are able to look back, on both the good and bad experiences and how they happened. It's also important you are able to draw the positives from the not so positive experiences, to see what lessons you can derive from your experiences.

ANTICIPATE

I anticipate my next move, not because I am always ready,

but because I know that if I don't, what I fail to anticipate can unexpectedly go wrong.

My mum would often say, 'Time and tide wait for no man,' and she was right. Time or issues don't wait for us. When we don't anticipate, or try to find a resolve on our issues, they have the potential to escalate and bring with them more concern, stress and uncertainty.

Issues and circumstances don't wait until we're emotionally or mentally ready to deal with them. And waiting on something and not being proactive can leave us with a fait accompli; not a fait accompli we wanted or were hoping for, but one that brings about a different outcome, usually one we weren't wanting, or expecting.

And as hard as it is for us to deal with things, it becomes harder when we don't at least try. But if we learn to anticipate and act on the things we need to deal with, things can get easier.

I learned through necessity and that is often how it starts. But the more we are in control of what we have to deal with, the less scary it is; although I appreciate it's hard at the time.

LESSONS IN DIVERSITY

Besides making the world a beautiful and interesting place, an important lesson is working with and accepting our diversity, because we are all different. We need to learn to be accepting of others, in the same way we dare

70

to be different. Our differences should be embraced.

We need to appreciate and embrace that we live in a diverse world. The world needs diversity for it to survive. To keep pace with the world's diversity, we should promote diversity in the way we perceive things.

We typically want everyone to be the way we want to see them, rather than the way they really are. Having a disability makes someone more unique, but having to mould into another person's version of how they want that person to be doesn't work and isn't right.

Diversity can be something we struggle to come to terms with; but we're all unique and different and being different means we are already diverse. Being honest, open and transparent should be all that matters. It is down to our particular mindset, how we see each other, how we see our lives and our world.

Understanding we are all different, handling differences effectively and being okay about it, is what we need to integrate successfully, and to bring more peace and harmony into our lives.

HOW TO DEVELOP MINDFULNESS

Mindfulness is the psychological process of purposely bringing attention to our experiences, occurring in the present moment without judgment.

Developing mindfulness allows us to feel and understand self-care and our emotions. This is the first step, because self-care means we're working on being self-aware. Learning to align ourselves with our internal thoughts allows our feelings to come to the surface, to identify our issues, so that we can start working to find a resolve, to get past them.

Mindfulness allows us to pay attention to what's happening in the present moment, without us passing judgment. It's a technique that helps us manage our thoughts, feelings and mental health.

To practice mindfulness, we need to first learn to put in place effective listening techniques, so that we spend more time finding or reaching an understanding, and less time feeling misunderstood. If used consistently, mindfulness can have a domino effect in other areas of our lives too. When we're grounded in the moment, it can also ease worry and anxiety.

Start by placing your feet on the floor and take a moment to notice your surroundings, what is going on around you. Close your eyes and notice the quiet.

Developing mindfulness means less stress, which means we're more likely to cope with life's challenges and make better decisions. It means we can spend less time focusing on the things we have little control over. Being mindful means we're also less likely to ruminate on issues, and increase working memory, so we have greater cognitive ability.

Mindfulness can be developed through the practice of meditation, or just spending time quietly in thought. Mindfulness is something we should continually work on if we are to have peace in our lives.

OUR CONSCIOUS CONNECTIONS

The more we're aware of and deal with our unconscious thoughts, the more we stay consciously connected. As children, we're not always equipped to make the conscious connections we need to make.

It is only when we reach adulthood and begin to look back on our childhood that we become aware and understand. Making conscious connections means we can analyse and deal with things and that needs to happen if we are going to change our perceptions and behaviour.

The subconscious is involuntary, it is the reasoning mind that remains in a dormant state, which we have no access to, unless we learn how to access it. The subconscious accepts what is impressed upon it. It stores all our experiences, until such a time those experiences emerge and take shape as an outer experience that corresponds to their content.

The subconscious doesn't reason like the conscious can. It doesn't dispute what it receives, it just takes what we give it. For our behaviour patterns to change, the subconscious and conscious need to work in sync.

Unless we are able to consciously stay in the moment, it is our subconscious thoughts and patterns that continue to guide our behaviour and, unless we are able to make ourselves aware of what lies beneath our conscious, we may fail to deal with our issues and our experiences.

MAKING THE CONNECTIONS

When we are not emotionally present, we may fail to make the connections between what we think and how we feel.

Traumatic experiences can prevent emotional development. Emotional pain brought about through trauma isn't always something we consciously recognise, and if we do, we may keep it to ourselves.

'Trauma isn't what happens to you, it's what happens inside you.' – Tim Ferriss. Although trauma happens to us, the biggest trauma is keeping the confusion and pain caused by our experiences to ourselves. Often, it is the silent battles that do us more harm than the trauma itself. The mind may often be distracted, it may be stuck in the past, or it may be focused on other things.

But a struggle in one area of our lives will spread into other areas, unless we're prepared to address and deal with the issues pertaining to those struggles. It is important we address our issues. Once we are able to address those, we can start to make the link between our past experiences, our issues and staying current. The issues we have to deal with are often the reason we are unable to emotionally move on with our lives.

With positive work on ourselves, emotional and spiritual growth can happen, but where time heals certain memories, other memories can keep us stuck. We can move forward with positivity, once we are able to address the things that need to be addressed.

DEEPER AWARENESS

We should be willing to transform ourselves, so that we can change the distorted energy patterns that often become the cause of disease, ageing and infirmity. Having deep awareness within ourselves is the key to renewal and change.

It is our inner thoughts that influence how we react to situations, but any transformation comes from the soul. Infinitely, it is the soul that gives us full access to our potential, it is the soul that brings more awareness to our lives past and present; the soul brings intelligence and creativity into every aspect of our lives.

When we commit to a deeper awareness, we transcend the obstacles that affect the mind and body in our everyday lives. Through deeper awareness, we may commit to our relationships on a more mature level.

It is often through deeper awareness of the soul that our actions tie us to a person, allowing us to bond with that person on a more soulful level.

EMOTIONAL STABILITY

As we continue to live our lives, emotional stability is something that we need to continually work at. Life's hurdles are inevitable. They're not something we can always plan for and are sometimes hard to comprehend and overcome.

But it is often our inability to deal with hurdles that can leave us in a position where we are less than able to cope, mentally and emotionally. In those circumstances, we may not always know how to come to terms with what we are dealing with and being angry is sometimes part of that process. Some of us may choose to block our experiences out, others may simply do their best to cope with what they have to deal with.

To work on emotional stability, we need to continue to find a level of acceptance and understanding on our experiences. We should work on the premise that the things we can change we will, and the things we can't change, we should try to accept.

THE FULLER PICTURE

It is often only when someone is no longer in our lives that we come to analyse and understand the reality of the relationship we had with that person. We may also come to realise that nothing would or could have ever changed, but we may still try to convince ourselves otherwise.

When we come to see the bigger picture in one area of our lives, we can get to see pictures in other areas of our lives too. Relationships are intertwined, so that when we're looking at one relationship, we're also looking at other relationships.

But sometimes being in the thick of it means we may not always see the fuller picture of our situation, or what we have to deal with. It is only when we look back retrospectively that we may understand and see; by which time it is often too late to change anything.

Other people being responsible for the roles they play paves the way for us to understand their roles; but we should only choose to own what is ours. Where we once may have had disappointment or anger, as we get older, and with work on ourselves, we should be able to get better at letting those go.

Our experiences are our experiences, we don't have to like them, and through intuitive understanding we can come to accept them. Having the fuller picture helps and that allows for emotional and spiritual growth.

ACKNOWLEDGING SUCCESS

Just because we choose to block things out, doesn't mean those things didn't happen, in the same way failing to acknowledge another person's success doesn't deny their success. Blocking anything out doesn't make it so.

When we block things out, we not only fail to recognise our own potential success, but other people's also. It is important we are happy for others.

Perhaps it isn't their success that's bothering us, perhaps it's our upbringing and our perceived lack of achievement. We may struggle to be happy for those who are more successful than we are, or who we perceive have more than we do.

Taking that stance is not the spiritual way. Instead, we need to learn to be charitable towards other people and their success, if we are going to recoup some of our own.

TRUST

A lack of trust can affect the strength of our social, mental, physical and emotional health. To have trust is to have faith that someone has our back. Where we fail to trust our judgment, or our gut instinct, we won't trust ourselves, therefore may resist trusting others.

Negative beliefs attach themselves to anyone who lacks trust in others, which means they're likely to attract similar people who reflect those same negative beliefs, rather than challenge them. Being around people who are distrustful is exhausting, especially when their distrust is tied to people and previous events.

Where our decisions do not concur with the universal principles, trust can become an issue and people may start to work against each other, and things may not work out.

We all have the ability to change and do things differently. We also need to have trust and respect because those attributes are an integral part of any relationship. We need to distinguish between healthy and unhealthy relationships and situations.

When we get trapped into feelings of indecision, inaction and distrust, those feed into our psyche, and into our relationships. It is important for others to have trust in us, and for us to have trust in others.

TRUST AND DOING WHAT'S RIGHT

We should all be taught from an early age to do what is right. Karma teaches us that we're accountable for ourselves and others too, therefore it's important we do what is right, even if others fail to do right by us.

Doing what is right is all about trust. When someone puts their trust in us and we let them down, it says more about us than it does about them. If we let someone down, it is important we go back in and correct what we've done.

Even if we choose to move on, we should remedy it first. As karma dictates, it is the right thing to do. Life works out better for us when we do.

LISTENING ATTENTIVELY

We listen to what we want to hear. If what we're being told doesn't concur with our own thoughts or beliefs, or how we see our lives, we may ignore what's being said.

We listen in order to reply because it would be rude for us not to, but we don't always listen enough for us to think deeply, or understand. Instead, we may work off our own understanding. If we're interested and it's something we want to hear, another person's opinion is something we might use, but we may ignore what other people say, and form our own opinions.

It also depends on personality. Some of us are automatically receptive to other people's opinions and advice, and some of us aren't; but perhaps that depends on the approach of the person handing out the advice.

Reading between the lines can teach us how to deal with issues in a way that allows us to explore our life, with its different outcomes. We shouldn't close our mind; instead, we should find a different way of thinking, which works for us. On the whole, life becomes easier when we listen, primarily because we're opening our minds to new possibilities, which helps us with personal, emotional and spiritual growth.

We should want to listen attentively, rather than superficially to people's words, because it shows we're interested and because it's the right thing to do. It also allows us to embrace new thoughts and ideas and that helps us learn about ourselves, other people and about change in the process.

TO UNDERSTAND, TO FORGIVE

Our ability to see beyond the hurt encourages emotional growth. When we understand other people's actions, we should find it easier to let go of resentment. We may never go on to experience life in its entirety if we don't let go of resentment. It's the act of letting go that allows us to make space for bigger and better things.

It is easy to hold on to resentment when others who have hurt us don't express remorse, accept what they've done, or apologise. But that is something for them to reconcile; instead we need to rationalise and understand.

When we carry a burden, we're causing ourselves more pain: when we stop inflicting hurt on ourselves, we start to encourage a shift in something bigger than ourselves. It is a statement that encourages understanding, resulting in emotional and spiritual growth and letting go.

BRINGING AWARENESS

Bringing awareness to our emotions brings reasoning where we didn't previously have it and, where we have reasoning, we can work on change.

Bringing awareness helps us recognise and understand how our emotions affect us, how our emotions help us interact with others and what impact our emotions have on other people's emotional state.

We should be conscious of our emotions, but that can be challenging for many reasons:

- We come to experience more than one emotion
- Emotions constantly change depending on what we're dealing with
- We block out our emotions, particularly if they're too painful
- There are times we need to become more aware of our

emotions particularly when we're under stress, but being under stress means we're more likely to ignore them

- We spend a considerable amount of time living in denial because we would rather not deal with our emotions

Although being in denial may seem a sign of weakness to others, it is often short-lived because denial, if not dealt with, can manifest itself in other ways. We may stall or ignore our emotions temporarily, but that will be short-lived, as we will need to deal with our emotions further down the line.

Being aware of our emotions is the first step to changing how we deal with our emotions.

FINDING OURSELVES

If I had advice to give anyone, it would be to know what you want from life, because not only will how you perceive yourself change, but so too will your whole outlook. I am not sure how many of us really get that close to knowing ourselves.

The simple, uncomplicated life, the spiritual life, doesn't seem to exist in this fast-paced world we live in. We forget who is important and what matters. We should try to find happiness in ourselves, our thoughts, and in the simple things. If we were to ask ourselves if we were happy, we might stumble to find the perfect answer.

Instead, as we go about our lives, we may look to find

happiness in material things, in our careers and with our families, but inwardly those things may never make us happy, unless we are innately happy. The best way for us to find happiness is to look at ourselves from the inside out.

It is not so much about finding silence, as paying attention to what is already there, through shifting our attention to the part of us that is constantly aware, the little voice inside of us that speaks. We should listen to the inner voice that is attached to an eternal presence that is constantly with us.

When we learn to anchor ourselves and channel our thoughts, we move with that rhythm and should become aware of the inner stillness that continues to support and sustain us in our conscious thinking.

UNDERSTANDING OUR WORTH

As a child, I didn't know I was dealing with or had a disability. I also didn't understand why I would start things and not finish them, and used to think that giving up meant I had no staying power. As an adult, and understanding myself now, I believe the opposite to be true.

When we choose to walk away, it has nothing to do with a lack of staying power or emotional weakness, and everything to do with how emotionally strong we are. When we choose to walk away because things aren't right, we know our worth; not because we need others to understand, or validate our worth. It shouldn't matter what others think.

Those who constantly pay attention to what other people think may lose sight of how strong they really are, and of their worth. We shouldn't have to prove or validate ourselves to anyone, nor should we have to convince others of our worth. Only what we know for ourselves.

FREE WILL

Free will is the power of acting without the constraints of fate or necessity, and our ability for us to act at our own discretion. Acting at our own discretion allows us to make our own choices, live independently, become self-sufficient and be more spontaneous.

Free will is also the ability to make our own decisions, the outcomes of which cannot be known in advance. Free will means choices and decisions are not predetermined, our ability to act according to our own free will and purpose.

Although our lives are mapped out for us long before we're born, we do have free will to make certain changes, once we're here. Not everyone will be born into a situation, or circumstance where free will is in abundance. For some, acts of free will are freer than for others. Some of us are born into families where free will is restricted, where our lives are dictated.

But in the pursuit of being able to make our own decisions through our own personal interests, we have free will to change certain things. When we have a lack of free will, we have little choice over our decisions.

Where attitudes, decisions and thoughts are influenced by culture, where decisions are established in advance and we're expected to fit into the norm long before we're born, those decisions are predetermined, and not free will.

BEING UNNECESSARILY DIFFICULT

There is a difference between being unnecessarily difficult because we can and know we'll get away with it, and being unnecessarily difficult because we struggle and fail to cope.

Those who are on the receiving end of unnecessarily difficult behaviour, may choose to ignore it in order to live a quiet life, so as not to rock the boat, and because in the short term it's easier; but in the longer term, unnecessarily difficult behaviour is something that never goes away, particularly if it's not dealt with. If we have someone in our lives that continually mirrors this behaviour, then it's time for us to let them go.

Also, it is generally accepted that if someone is struggling with something, they're being difficult and it's usually a one-off, then that's okay; but being difficult for difficult's sake is never okay. Dealing with any conflict takes energy, patience, maturity and experience.

In those situations, it is important we are able to stand back, so that we can work on being objective, calm and dispassionate. When it comes to unnecessarily difficult behaviour, we can choose not to have those people in our lives.

PERSONAL BOUNDARIES

Personal boundaries are the ones we work our lives around, the boundaries we create for ourselves that we hope others will abide by.

Boundaries are there to tell others what they can and can't expect from us, and what we should expect from them. We may put personal boundaries in place to protect us from people who can be demanding, controlling, pushy or abusive.

The most common of boundaries are:

PHYSICAL BOUNDARIES

Physical boundaries apply to our personal space, our bodies and our privacy.

EMOTIONAL BOUNDARIES

Emotional boundaries are the boundaries we use to separate our responsibility and emotions from another person's boundaries. Emotional boundaries are healthy boundaries that protect us from feeling guilty about another person's problems, or negative feelings. These boundaries also help us negate and prevent us taking other people's comments personally.

Healthy emotional boundaries require clear internal boundaries; internal boundaries that involve feelings and responsibilities to ourselves and other people.

MENTAL BOUNDARIES

Mental boundaries apply to our opinions and values. If we are gullible, our mental boundaries aren't clear enough. If we find it hard to hold on to our opinions, or are easily coerced or swayed into another person's thinking, our mental boundaries are weak. There is also a suggestion that if we are argumentative or defensive, we also have weak boundaries.

SPIRITUAL BOUNDARIES

Spiritual boundaries relate to beliefs that connect us to a higher power, helping us to nurture a spiritual life. Boundaries are our rules. The hard part is making sure others respect our boundaries and don't cross them.

OUR INNER CHILD

Our inner child may always be affected by our early experiences. If we're told we're useless, we may begin to believe we're useless, in the same way if we're told we're not loved, we may begin to question our ability to love, and be loved. On a subconscious level, our experiences can begin to affect our relationships. Years of being around other people's behaviour, or feeling unloved, may stay stored in our subconscious and eventually play out through our conscious.

It is often only when we come to question our lives, or begin to understand other people's issues and decisions, that we realise those issues aren't ours to carry. Often, the issues we carry result from the effects of other people's decisions, how those decisions make us feel, and how we may react to those feelings.

As we begin to deal with, and work through our experiences, we should slowly begin to fill with compassion, love and understanding. We should then begin to see that our inner child is special, that our inner child is loved, and it is capable of love.

When we love our inner child, we love ourselves. When we give hope back to our inner child, we give hope back to ourselves.

UNDERSTANDING YOUR EMOTIONS

Getting to know your emotions and understanding what they mean is the kindest thing you can ever do. It is the difference between staying well and becoming unwell.

Although emotions can add energy and a variety of feelings, which can have a positive impact on our lives, emotions can also leave us flat; particularly when we struggle to understand what they mean.

We are either in control of our emotions, or we are controlled by them, there is no half measure. They can either help us spiritually grow, or they can leave us feeling confused. Our emotions also have the capacity to help us heal. When we learn and understand our emotions, we can stay well and present.

With all emotions, it is important we learn to identify the message behind them. If we're anxious, we need to ask why, or what we're anxious about. If we are angry, we need to look at why we are angry, come to understand that anger, anything that will help us unlock and decipher our emotions.

Problems arise when we bury a lot of what we feel, because we can't face up to dealing with our emotions, we don't like confrontation, or we're in denial that our emotions exist. But we can't deal with our emotions when we don't understand, therefore the key to unlocking our emotions is to understand where they come from, or why we have them.

QUIET CONTEMPLATION

I often use quiet contemplation as a tool to strive for inner peace. Our inner perceptions represent peace, how we deal with our lives, and the people in it.

Inner peace comes from how we think about ourselves, how we deal with our issues and how we deal with life. It represents quietness; a quietness that incorporates love and respect that we have for each other, despite any political, cultural and religious views.

Peace isn't about having a new car, or a big house. It isn't about looking at what other people have and wanting what they have, or the latest electronic gizmo; material worth gives us nothing. It can also never guarantee peace or happiness. It is our perceptions that dictate our ability to be happy, and to find inner peace.

I often sit quietly and contemplate, as I look at my cat. When I think that her full tummy, somewhere warm for her to sleep and a hug is all she needs, she brings a smile to my face. I have always cherished the simple things in life.

NOT BEING RESENTFUL

When we can live with something traumatic or upsetting and no longer feel resentment, we know we have come through the healing process to a more spiritual existence.

That's not to say we won't have difficult days, but any feelings we do have should only be temporary. We need to continue to find a genuine understanding of the healing and spirituality process, and make better choices to support our understanding. It is important we are not resentful.

We should learn to embrace the happy times and let go of the painful memories that can make us feel irritated or upset. It may take more effort to consciously work through the process, but it will be worth the effort if it puts us into a better mental and emotional space.

A LIFE WITH INTEGRITY

If I could impress upon others the importance of incorporating one value into their lives, that value would be integrity.

Integrity should be the backbone to humanity, because it gives our lives purpose. It makes for good character, which is extremely important. When we use integrity consistently, it becomes the norm and part of who we are. When we have integrity, we're honest and have strong moral principles.

Integrity examples include:

- Saying you're going to do something and following it through even if you have to make the extra effort
- Remaining true to your values, your friends and family
- Not talking about people behind their back
- Not betraying anyone's trust
- Taking responsibility and owning up to your mistakes
- Not allowing someone else to take the flack for something you've done
- Keeping something that you're told in confidence to yourself
- Finding something, knowing who it belongs to and handing it back
- Not telling white lies to get yourself out of trouble
- Not moving the boundaries just so it suits you

Having integrity allows for maturity and can help lead to a more peaceful life. It allows us to follow our moral and ethical convictions, without needing to find a compromise, where doing the right thing becomes the norm, is second nature and instrumental for emotional and spiritual growth.

STANDING BY YOUR MORALS

Defining, living with, and communicating your core values will mean nothing if those values don't push you towards living better lives.

When I look back on my childhood, it wasn't the things mum said once that were of the most value, but the things she continually repeated. Morals are to be frequently used if they are to become part of us.

Unless we continue to reinforce our core values, those values will be of little significance to us, or anyone else. They show others what we stand for, they guide us on a more spiritual path, and ultimately become our legacy when we're no longer around.

WHY WE NEED HUMILITY

Humility is the act of being modest, it is the opposite of being arrogant. It is part of being spiritual. We can never successfully forge ahead without it.

Since everything we do is based on how we act and react, we should try to act and react with humility. It makes what we put out there real. Humility helps build trust between people; in families, in society, between continents and in the world.

Nelson Mandela said, 'The first thing is to be honest with yourself.' Without honesty, you can't make the right impact on society. Humility, integrity, respect and honesty formed the foundation to Nelson Mandela's life. He was a huge inspiration and I was fortunate to see him speak in person.

Humility teaches us how to behave, and yet it is a trait that may be continually overlooked. Humility is the quality of being humble. Those who are humble put others before themselves, and think of others first. It doesn't mean they neglect themselves; it just means they're happy to think about and help others who need the help before them. Having humility also means not drawing attention to yourself. It's a good trait to have.

Humility helps us respect each other and other people's opinions. Humility is selfless. It is living in accordance with truth and realising we have much to be thankful for. With humility, we understand we are no more important than the next person, that we are all equal and valuable. It matters, because we all have the right to be treated and spoken to in the same way. There isn't enough humility in the world.

Without acting on and using humility, it will be impossible to recognise that everyone has an equal right to be heard, or for us to listen to others openly.

LIVING WITH HUMILITY

Our past is responsible for shaping the way we see and live our lives in the present, for some of us that becomes a humbling experience, for others it can be extremely difficult.

Without bringing spirituality into our lives, it may be difficult for us to achieve humility, value our lives and other people. It is the spiritual existence that brings about empathy, compassion and tolerance and it is those things that give us humility.

Regardless of how we grow up, and how our lives have previously been shaped, we can all live our lives with humility, so that we can learn to appreciate the things we take for granted, the little things, and the things we've got, or might want.

When we grow up with very little, it is easier to demonstrate a more humbling existence and attitude, but as adults, it can also throw us into a 'must have' mentality, where we may stop at nothing until we get what we want.

HUMILITY AND INCLUSION

One of my favourite quotes is from the film *Chocolat*, when Father Henri, the village priest in the sleepy hamlet in which the film is based, delivers his weekly sermon. In an indirect reference to the outsider who has challenged the villagers' religious beliefs and norms, he tells his parishioners that they cannot measure how good they are by what they don't do, or who they choose to exclude, but rather by what they embrace and who they choose to include.

This resonates with how I live my life. Ever since I was a small child, I never felt the need to prove myself. I was never full of my own self-importance; I was grateful and respectful.

Humility is something we can all have, but not all of us will. Our lives are measured by it, how we behave, and how we choose to relate to other people. A humble person goes about their life in an understated fashion, instead of being pompous and self-opinionated.

Although our experiences help us mature and come to terms with many aspects of our lives, being humble allows us to deal with our issues without other people having to know our business and without a fuss.

We come to accept praise gracefully, without others needing to know we have been praised. Humility helps us listen to others and, in doing so, places others before ourselves.

With humility we're happy to think about other people who may need our help. It means that everything we do comes from a gentle, more considerate and conciliatory place. We may live life at a much slower pace and choose a life that's more purposeful. Even where there are differences in the world, a person with humility chooses not to see a difference, and continues to act with humility.

Unfortunately, even if we start off being humble, in a society that encourages us to be less individual and more inclusive, it can be hard to stay that way: but we should at least try. Humility concurs with the universe and is a good way for us to live.

GREATER SELF-AWARENESS

It doesn't matter who we are, or who we go on to meet, everyone has something special to give. On our part, we should be open enough to receive it.

Every encounter gives us the opportunity to become more self-aware, by showing us what we can accept about ourselves. Our behaviour gives information to other people, which is why first impressions count.

The key to greater self-awareness lies in what we can learn about ourselves, and how we may accept ourselves and our shortcomings. For example, someone says something about us, and it hits a nerve because we know they're speaking the truth.

In that situation, it may be hard for us to acknowledge our flaws, let alone hear others point them out. The same point can be applied to almost any situation. Our reactions are simply a reflection of how we judge ourselves, and how we feel about ourselves.

It also depends on who we're talking to. We may start to judge when we feel we're being emotionally threatened in some way, particularly if we're in the company of, or living with someone who is dictatorial, and we're living with resentment.

Although we very rarely understand it, judgments are usually based on our own emotional reactions and, when applied appropriately, help us gain an insight into how we think and behave.

We should explore all assumptions and beliefs. How we judge others acts as a mirror, so that we get to see how we present ourselves.

WORKING ON OUR CORE VALUES

Unless we walk a mile in another person's shoes, we can never know what they struggle with, but that shouldn't stop us wanting to help.

It goes back to our core values and what we're taught as children. Core values are the fundamental beliefs of a person, the beliefs we hold close to us that we use in our everyday lives; core values such as empathy, respect, compassion, honesty and trust. We don't start out with empathy or compassion, but we can develop these qualities if we choose.

Putting others first shows others we're selfless, as long as we're doing it for good reason, or it may be an attention-seeking, or approval issue. We may learn from a young age that the way for us to gain approval from others is for us to do what they want.

If more of us were selfless, we'd all be better people, living better lives and the world would be safer. We would give back. Putting others first doesn't mean we deny ourselves of our own needs, we can do both. If our core values are at the heart of how we live our lives, and how we behave in our relationships, those relationships will thrive.

We should want to be selfless. It should be instinctive in all of us, part of our core values and a sense of who we are. Sadly, it seems that some people's core values have continued to decrease over the years and we need to do more to turn that around.

GOOD MORAL VALUES

We all have and live by different moral values, codes of conduct, which can either be the making, or the breaking of us.

Incorporating good moral values into our everyday lives gives us clarity and focus and a good sense of self, as long as we continue to live and abide by them. Those same values can also go on to give us positive results in other areas of our lives.

We should consistently incorporate good moral values into all areas of our personal and working lives. The more we practise, the better we can be and the better we can be with others. The world we live in would be better too.

USING INTROSPECTION

My thoughts are never far away from my unconscious thinking. But introspection isn't a one-minute wonder. It is something that needs to be continuously honed.

We know what introspection is, but why should we use it? We should use it because without the examination or observation of our own emotional and mental processes, we may never emotionally or spiritually grow, nor can we learn to look within ourselves and our lives.

Without introspection, we may never know what it means to contemplate, what it means to ponder; to reflect, nor what it is to be thoughtful. We may never know mediation, meditation, or how to use reflection.

Introspection can be used at any time, it's easy to do and doesn't take a lot of effort. To get started you need to sit and focus on one particular thing that's bothering you. Quiet introspection can be extremely valuable. Introspection can help us think about our lives, what certain things mean, and how we feel about them. Introspection, if used frequently and consistently, means we can begin to hear the little voice inside our head talk back at us, with positive affirmation.

Introspection helps us revisit our experiences, so that we understand how they fit into our lives. It allows us to deal with our issues, which then allows for personal and spiritual growth.

WHY WE MUSTN'T BE DEFINED

We define ourselves by the standards we create. Those standards are a checklist of our ethics, morality and behaviour.

Our lives contain a set of standards, initially set by our parents, by which we continue to define ourselves. The problem is that most of us don't think about the standards we're subconsciously living by, even though we may still be defined by them.

It is a checklist we adopt, through our family, our environment, our friends, through our culture, and our beliefs. When it comes to Western culture, we are often defined by comparison to others, how we look, and through material gain.

We are also defined by our exam success, by our careers, by how many rungs of the corporate ladder we've climbed. Our self-worth is based on monetary and materialistic gain.

We should learn to ignore how others define us, or how we define ourselves; we are not our attachments. Instead, we should consciously be aware of people and things that influence us, and understand how each of those influences work. As long as those influences are positive, we can change for the positive through emotional and spiritual growth.

Sadly, there will always be certain influences that affect how we behave and how we feel, how we define ourselves, and those may set us up to fail. When we define ourselves by things that are outside of our control, we may also fail.

We need to find satisfaction in ourselves, and in our lives, and not be defined by a checklist of standards.

SALT OF THE EARTH

Not everyone will be honest, trustworthy and reliable, but these are values we should all strive for. Respect, honesty and living with good moral values should be something we all aspire to. People with these values are good people, they are 'the salt of the earth'.

For many, scientific improvements and advances in technology are enhancing our way of life, but we're still not getting our interpersonal relationships right. We may not improve ourselves; instead we may often fail to show respect to each other and to our different values. We should all aim to be 'the salt of the earth'.

Our accomplishments have simply provided ways to demonstrate our differences, often in ignorance of the fact that we should work together for the greater good, and for our place in the world.

Instead, we need to go back to basics and work on improving our moral and spiritual compass, think about our mental and emotional health, and how we can change for the better.

RUNNING AWAY

As we continue to protect ourselves by mentally running away, we may become more exposed.

To other people, our lives may appear perfect and we may appear perfect, but we know deep down that our emotions and our lives are far from it. We may continue to run from our issues, from ourselves, or from our lives. We may also subconsciously run from anyone who is more successful than us. But whilst we may live in denial, we continually expose ourselves to the trauma we've previously experienced.

It is not so much that we ignore our truth, others may do this and we may live our life the way they want us to, instead and until we come to piece our own life together that is our life. Also, when we count someone else's blessings instead of our own, we may make ourselves more vulnerable. We may choose denial, so that we don't have to face the truth. But we need to face our truth.

Ironically, as we run from ourselves and our thoughts, we cut ourselves off from our experiences, the very things that can help us understand and live happier lives.

WHY IT'S GOOD TO INTERNALISE

It is important we are able to internalise our thoughts, not because we're manic or self-obsessed, but because it helps us understand our life, and express our feelings.

Not everyone who internalises knows how to express how they feel; so, understanding how to internalise (to absorb an idea and accept) is a good place to start. Internalising how we feel helps us identify our issues.

In a world and environment that can often bring uncertainties, internalising our thoughts can generate new understanding. Being able to interpret our feelings can also help us understand our lives more, our childhood more, and can make our lives easier.

It is a safe place in our head where we can go, one that doesn't judge, a place that's without interference. It is a place that knows us, a place we're comfortable with.

Without internalising, we may never understand why things happen the way they do. The more we internalise; the more we can understand, the more we can come to terms with and accept, the more we can let things go.

FULL CIRCLE

Have you ever noticed how, after a series of events, the same situation you started with still exists, and you end up back at the place you chose to walk away from?

Even if we don't believe in how the universe works, what is meant to happen will always finds its way back. Coming full circle brings us back to that place, and whatever we were in doubt about comes full circle if that was the road we were meant to take.

Life has a way of balancing and correcting. Feeling and being positive can have a positive outcome on timings, and the decisions we make. If we choose to see something positive, we see it as positive, in the same way we may choose to see something as negative. There is essentially no good or bad, negative or positive, just how we choose to see things.

The things we see as bad seem to take longer to work

through than the good. There will be lots of twists and turns, we just need to understand them. We also need to understand that we are where we are supposed to be, at any given time.

We shouldn't fight against things coming full circle. Knowing this simply empowers us to understand the changes we need to make, so we can see the people and patterns that are occurring, and so that we can bring about a different outcome, one that serves us better.

NO NEED TO FEEL GUILTY

We may reflect on our relationships in certain times more than others, often around the time when someone we love is terminally ill. Relationships are usually about expression and we have to be able to express ourselves.

It would be easy to look back on those times and feel guilty about something we've said or done, and get cross with ourselves, but it's unhelpful and counterproductive. We shouldn't have to respond differently to someone because they are terminally ill. It is perfectly acceptable to react to something we're not happy with. What we want to say shouldn't change.

CONTENTMENT

Contentment comes with living a content life. Contentment comes when you have everything you need emotionally, and you're at peace and at ease with yourself.

To have contentment we need to understand and deal with our issues and experiences, and come to terms with our past. It is also important we come to understand what our purpose is, why we're here and why the life we have is the one meant for us. Contentment is also looking at the little things, without wanting or needing the bigger things and living in the moment.

We shouldn't let aggression or jealousy in because they can interfere with contentment. These are major factors of discontentment, which, if you have for too long, can eventually leave scars on your soul.

OUR INTUITIVE GUIDE

As a child, if I would have had an understanding of what intuition was, I would have had an insight into my difficulties with my mental and emotional struggles. I understand more about my intuition now. Now I use it as my guide.

With it, I would have had the chance to focus more positively without constantly looking back on my non-achievements and feeling guilty about them.

It is our intuition that keeps our lives centred, so that we can understand why our lives turn out the way they do. When we come to understand why something happens the way it does, we can bring acceptance and closure.

How well our intuition works very much depends

on how much we practice listening to our thoughts and being open to that little voice inside our head. Intuition is something we can all access, but some of us may not always know, or understand how to do so.

The more we are able to use our intuition, the more attention we can pay to our inner thoughts, the more we can rely on those thoughts to correct what we need to change.

FINDING INNER CALM

Working towards inner calm is something we should all continue to do.

Inner calm represents an inner quietness, a quietness that allows us to see ourselves as we are. It's a journey of self-discovery and understanding of shared experiences. We know we are calm when the mind is free of aggression, free of simple frustrations and stressful tendencies. Inner calm helps us seek out the simple pleasures in life.

People who possess these qualities are able to handle difficult situations, with a knowing that those situations should pass. They are more aware and accepting of themselves and can take things in their stride.

We should find inner calm when we stop drawing ourselves into conflict, stop passing judgment and putting conflict out to others. Following a spiritual path paves the way for us to achieve inner calm; managing it means we will have a more peaceful demeanour about us.

Having inner calm gives us a deep appreciation of our experiences, of the world and what everything means. It also means we can have empathy, compassion and tolerance; things we should all try to strive for.

OUR INTERNAL WORKINGS

Our emotions have everything to do with our internal workings, but unless we deal with our 'emotional cognitive framework', which comprises our emotional understanding of the world, of ourselves and other people, what we try to achieve may never work.

We can never expect to make headway and important decisions, without dealing with our emotions first. Our emotions are responsible for what we think about ourselves, they govern our behaviour, how we communicate, how well we adapt into our lives and how easily we go on to make those all-important decisions.

We will always have uncertainties and lack clarity around our choices when we struggle with our emotions. We cannot expect to function well unless we understand and put our emotions in order first.

OUR JOURNEY

Our journey is ours to make and should never be compared to another's. For some it may happen almost immediately, for others it may take time. What matters is that we finish our journey, not where we start it, or where we've come from.

As one door closes, another door opens. The message is simple. Our journey is for us to complete, just don't give up.

LIVING LIFE WITH PURPOSE

If you're fortunate enough to have support that helps you live your life with purpose, you should always try to make yourself and your life better.

If you have never been encouraged to think outside the box, to think about life and what you want from it, you may never know what you're capable of. What drives you as a child is different to what drives you as an adult, unless that purpose is already within you.

Whatever your purpose, it may often come when you least expect, in the shape of an opportunity, or a sign you didn't see before. A purpose isn't something we should force.

TIME TO THINK

As a child, I would often retreat into my own little world. I was comfortable in my own headspace; I was happy there.

As children, we are not equipped to understand or solve our problems, but as adults we are expected to problem solve, whether we feel we're equipped or not. Instinctively, the biggest problem for many of us is the application. Also, the problem is our perspective and where we are in our headspace. We need to give ourselves time to think.

As we grow, we all have issues that we deal with, but they need to be solved and we need to be instrumental in solving them. Often, because it's too difficult, we may ignore the fact those issues need clarification, or solution.

When we're in a good headspace we are capable of working things out, even the things we may have failed to accomplish before. But running away can make us feel empowered, if only for a finite time; particularly if we're actively choosing not to focus on the present.

When we don't have to think of what is going on in the here and now it helps, but things tucked away in our unconscious may only become problems when they come back into our conscious thinking.

Problems don't exist in the place we arrive at, while we're ignoring them. We have a new focus and feel good because we've temporarily made it that way.

Inevitably, without sorting our problems out we may begin to trip up, first on the little things, then eventually on the bigger things, until they can no longer be ignored, or contained.

POSITIVE COMMUNICATION

It matters that how we say what we say resonates with people in positive ways; positive communication matters.

When we disregard another person's healthy emotional pathways and use pull downs to communicate instead, it says a lot about us and where we are with our own emotions.

If we want other people's words to be positive and encouraging towards us, our words need to be met in the same way towards them. We should look in the mirror at our reflection, to see how we're communicating, so that what we say and how what we say it is positive.

WORKING AT RELATIONSHIPS

In our less than perfect world, being taken for granted seems to have become par for the course. Sadly, for some of us, once a relationship beds in, complacency also sets in.

When we're not coping, those close to us usually get the brunt of our feelings. Where we're not connecting, or don't know why we feel what we feel, we can lose control of how we respond to those around us.

Our behaviour is mirrored through our subconscious thoughts. Like a story in a book that unfolds, the more positive our past, the more positive our thoughts, the better our behaviour is. With loved ones, we assume they'll stick around, regardless of how we treat them. We don't stop to think about how fortunate we really are.

The bond between us can emotionally grow stronger when we work on giving and receiving and, as a consequence of that, our relationships will flourish. Respect is something earned. We all need to feel valued and loved. It is important we work at our relationships.

THE PEANUT BUTTER FALCON

Have you ever come across a film that speaks to you, that makes you question your values, captures your soul and heightens your imagination? For me, *The Peanut Butter Falcon* is that film. It has the ability to help you change the way you see life.

The film is about Zak, a young man with Down's syndrome who escapes from an assisted living facility where he lives, to follow his dream of training to be a professional wrestler.

While on the run he makes an unlikely friendship with a fisherman who is also running away. As the two men embark on an adventure to find Zak's wrestling hero, they form an unlikely bond, a bond that turns into a beautiful friendship, whilst being chased by Zak's social worker, whose intention is to send Zak back into care. As the story unfolds, she begins to question her own values through Zak's eyes, and decides to take Zak's journey with him.

Just like the rest of us, Zak has dreams. He wants to be treated with inclusivity in the same way as everyone else; he wants to be accepted in a world that isn't always accepting of people who are different, and who deal with a disability. *The Peanut Butter Falcon* not only reminds us of disability in its wider context, but it also shows us there can be kindness, compassion and understanding for those of us who deal with a disability.

I resonated with this wonderful film for two reasons; I too live with a disability and it reminds me of the stigmas and prejudices I, like others with a disability, continue to face in our everyday lives, in what is an able-bodied world. The reality for anyone with a physical, mental or emotional disability is that we don't automatically fit in, although we hope others will allow us to.

This film highlights disability and what it feels like to live with one, but also highlights that disability shouldn't define us. It serves to remind us that we are all the same, that each of us should strive to ensure everyone is inclusive, not exclusive, and to bring understanding where disability may not always be seen in this way.

For me, this film not only captured my imagination with its story of adventure, but it also tugged at my heart strings. It shows us we can become kinder and be better people, and that we can all choose to make a difference to those who simply need that difference to be made.

WORKING WITH THE UNIVERSE

As a child growing up, I couldn't know why I struggled to get past the starting block in school, why I had mental and emotional challenges, why I dealt with anxiety, or why I couldn't motivate myself. But even with those issues, I was always instinctively aware I was attached to something bigger.

Looking back, I believe the universe was protecting me, watching over me, and it has brought me to this place. I innately lived with hope that one day I would find out about my disability, about my mental and emotional struggles. I never gave up on hope.

I believe that even if we're not aware, or we choose not to make ourselves aware of the universe, it is there, and we should work with it. Every internal thought process we have, we're putting those thoughts out to the universe. The universe is continuously aware.

The higher power, (something greater than us, like the universe) that surrounds our every thought and our every move, should continue to be part of our lives. It is important we work in alignment with what the universe needs, and expects from us. For us to succeed at life, we need to work with each other, and in harmony with the universe.

SOULMATES

You've probably heard it said many times before, 'I've met my soulmate', but its meaning may not have really registered. Or perhaps it's something that has unconsciously registered, but never really been consciously considered. That can happen too. Some of us may, on the other hand, already have an idea of what a soulmate is, or what a soulmate is supposed to be.

If you're in a soulmate relationship, you should never

have to wonder if that person is your soulmate. A soulmate is someone you're around or live with, who changes your outlook on life. A soulmate is someone you have a deep soul attraction with. An instant knowing that this is the person you want to spend the rest of your life with. It's an uplifting of the spirit that connects both the body and soul. Soulmates want the same things and are on the same path. They have the same desires, the same wants and needs.

A soulmate is someone you instantly have a connection with, and in some cases it isn't your first connection. You feel comfortable with that person; you want to spend time with that person, and feel unhappy when you're not with them. A soulmate wants to learn and grow with you on an emotional and spiritual level.

It is someone you want to spend the rest of your life with. A soulmate can also be someone you're not physically in a relationship with, but the depth of the connection you have with that person lasts a lifetime.

It is someone you can relate to and can resonate with, someone you feel comfortable talking to without feeling drained or threatened by what they say. Not everyone will find their romantic soulmate and that is okay. Many of us may not initially have a deep or natural affinity with our life partners.

What is important is that we are realistic about love and what it takes for us to nurture love in our relationships.

CHAPTER 4

HEALING AND SPIRITUALITY

'The spiritual life does not remove us from the world but leads us deeper into it.'

HENRI J. M. NOUWEN

Healing and spirituality are inseparable. With a healthy lifestyle we can be more open to the idea of being spiritual. Being spiritual allows for emotional and spiritual growth. Spirituality can help us become more empathetic, compassionate, tolerant, and understanding, and can open us up to a richer and fuller life.

It can also give us a deeper meaning and understanding to life, and help strengthen the connections between our intuition, our inner wisdom and ourselves. Being connected to our inner wisdom, in turn, helps us live a life of gratitude, which can promote healing.

FEELING GOOD ABOUT WRITING

I never associated my writing with autism, I never saw it as an autism trait, or a gift. As a child, I now understand it was the reason why I would start things and not finish them.

Through my daily blog, and for the first time, I have been able to bring my experiences to life. I talk about how I feel, about my experiences. My blog helps me understand my disabilities, it helps me understand my mental and emotional struggles, it also helps me cope with anxiety, which I didn't know I had as a child. It helps me mentally and emotionally heal.

My blog centres around my mental health and allows me to think about and bring clarity to my experiences, to my life. Writing about my struggles brings understanding into what has been a traumatic, and at times a confusing life.

It also helps others understand what they deal with, so they too can heal. My writing makes me feel good, it brings about a confidence in me; it helps me to know that I'm not alone. When an obsession has the potential to spill over and single me out, I take time for other things.

Through writing, I am doing something that I love that makes me feel better. Having impaired emotions breaks the cycle of it turning into an obsession. It's a feel-good factor. Writing empowers me to want to write more, to be more comfortable about my experiences.

My blog brings clarity where I didn't have it, and understanding where I had none. Through my writing, most of my issues are resolved; and I am able to heal.

Even if my enthusiasm were to seem like an obsession, I would never stop doing something that makes me and others feel better.

MENTAL AND PHYSICAL WELL-BEING

The World Health Organization (WHO) defines health as 'a state of complete physical, mental and social well-being and not merely the absence of disease or infirmity'.

Good physical health is linked to fitness, and emotional health is linked to personal well-being, feeling positive about yourself and in turn feeling positive about others.

Good emotional health means managing our emotions, recognising and managing the factors that affect our emotions and being able to express how we feel.

Mental and physical well-being are inseparable. Poor physical health can lead to an increased risk of developing mental health problems. Similarly, poor mental health can have an impact on our physical health, leading to an increased risk of disease.

If we are to struggle less with ill health, it is important we think about mental and physical well-being together, in its entirety, and work on both simultaneously. We cannot expect to be physically well if our mental and emotional states are poor.

Lifestyle factors will also influence the state of our mental and physical well-being.

NATURAL STRESS REMEDIES

The more we avoid moods and stress, the more our quality of life can improve.

Exercise is a good stress reliever that helps transport oxygen around the body. It is a natural mood lifter as it releases feel good hormones, so that we can feel more mentally alert and well. Exercise makes us feel good about ourselves, and can make us feel happier and healthier in the longer term.

Sunlight is also another health booster. Sunlight boosts chemicals in the brain, known as melatonin and dopamine, which make us feel more mentally alert. It not only provides us with Vitamin D, but also benefits us mentally. If we feel mentally alert, we're more likely to carry less anxiety and feel less depressed.

A healthy breakfast is a great way to start the day. Try to eat small, frequent meals, including vegetables, fruit and oily fish such as salmon, sardines, tuna and herring. Vitamin B, which is a natural energy/mood booster, should also be included. Other mood-boosting foods include green leafy vegetables, sweetcorn, berries, wholegrain cereals, brown rice and liver.

The more junk food we consume, the more we are likely to suffer from mood swings and depression, than if we try to eat healthily. We should also cut down, or cut out refined foods and sugar, limit the amount of caffeine, or fizzy drinks and alcohol we consume, and avoid stimulants such as cigarettes and drugs, as these can affect moods, and may lead to depression.

Having a pet also helps reduce stress. By reducing our stress, we are more likely to avoid mood swings and depression. Sleeping well is also a good recipe to avoid feeling irritable. If you are not tired and irritable, you are more likely to avoid the inevitable mood swings.

Getting our quota of sleep helps us to cope better in our day, and it also helps us avoid heart disease. Talk to a trusted friend, family member, doctor or a counsellor if you think you are emotionally, or mentally struggling.

CAPABLE OF CHANGE

We are all capable of change and in many cases we can, but not everyone knows how to change, or how to put their 'house in order'.

Fixing our lives can be painful, it is difficult sometimes, and requires essential change in how we look at things and how we choose to expend our energy. Some may look for help and not change, some may look for help and draw blanks, finding it difficult to make the link between their problems and their life. It's not always easy for us to know how to turn our lives around.

Admitting to something may seem easy, but it also depends on what we're admitting to. When our values become destructive and we repeat bad habits, it's not something we may recognise and, if we do, we may not feel comfortable admitting to; but it may often be clear to others that we have lost our way.

We are all capable of pulling it back, changing and living a more spiritual life.

STOP COMPARING YOURSELF

Always try to be better than you were yesterday. Stop focusing on, or being worried that you won't measure up and fail to recognise that you have something to give.

We may spend a large chunk of our lives trying to determine whether we stack up, when in reality there should be no ranking measure at all. Instead, we should measure up to our own personal potential.

Also, seeing ourselves as superior, or inferior doesn't work. These assessments can never be factually accurate, because individually we're not alike. We all come from different environments and backgrounds, our strengths and weaknesses may be different, we have different talents, therefore measuring ourselves against each other is not a fair evaluation.

Everyone is exactly equal in importance in the world. When you take away the ego, we are all exactly the same. We need to start by recognising that being the best at something only relates to us. If we have to rank ourselves, we need to do it against our own performance, and on our own future potential.

EMBRACING CHANGE

Change has to happen if we are to allow for spiritual and emotional growth. Throughout our lives, we may either welcome and learn to embrace change, or we may spend our time trying to avoid it, in the hope we may never have to make decisions that incorporate change.

The irony is that we can never avoid change; it comes whether we embrace it or not. The reason why change is hard, is because we emulate and follow patterns fixed from our childhood that we don't stop to question, or try to understand. If we are not encouraged to think about change, we may find it hard to change.

Change also creates uncertainty. It is human nature to want to go against the things that bring uncertainty. To deal with change we need to be confident and be open to the possibilities of change.

Being open-minded not only helps us have more understanding, but in turn more understanding helps us embrace the idea of change. When we get to a place where we feel the need for change, then we are ready to think about and embrace change.

There are people who don't embrace change because they're less open to new experiences, and because they're afraid of the potential chaos that change may bring to their daily routines. To think about change, we need to approach it with a different attitude. That doesn't mean we may never change our thinking, presently or otherwise.

It is our attitude that keeps us stuck and set in our ways.

When we open our minds to life and its possibilities, we are more likely to embrace the concept of change and change itself.

WORLD SUICIDE PREVENTION DAY

Mental health issues are something that we may all deal with at one time or another. To prevent us feeling worthless, useless, and to prevent us feeling suicidal, it is important to deal with our mental health and make that our number one priority.

Suicide is among the top twenty leading causes of death globally, for people of all ages. Annually, it is responsible for over 800 000 deaths, which equates to one suicide every forty seconds. For every death, twenty-five people make a suicide attempt and many more have serious thoughts of suicide.

For every suicide, approximately 135 people suffer intense grief, or are otherwise affected. This amounts to 108 million people per year who are profoundly impacted by suicidal behaviour.

Preventing suicide is possible: World Suicide Prevention Day is held annually on 10th September. It aims to raise awareness about mental health issues, to provide information to educate about the causes of suicide, and the warning signs to look out for. Every year, organisations and communities around the world come together to raise awareness of how we can create a world where fewer people die by suicide. This has been in place since 2003 and is recognised in around forty countries globally.

Each year has a different theme and focus, to bring to light a specific aspect of suicide prevention. At the time of writing, the present theme is 'Working Together to Prevent Suicide', chosen as it highlights the most essential ingredient for effective global suicide prevention and collaboration.

Research suggests that suicide prevention efforts are much more effective if they cover multiple levels and incorporate multiple interventions and this may often involve family, friends, healthcare professionals, co-workers, community members, schools, universities, and religious leaders.

As the statistics show, this isn't happening enough, but with help and support we can bring those numbers down.

If you are struggling with mental health issues, or you know someone else who is, please think about and ask for help. (Source: Samaritans.org & IASP.info)

HEALING CONFLICT FROM WITHIN

Conflicts are an inevitable part of life. However hard we try, it isn't always possible to avoid them, but the stronger we are mentally, the more comfortable we are at handling conflicts, often without having to cut ties.

When we choose to walk away, it is often because we are afraid to look deeply within ourselves. We bury the things we don't want to deal with or don't like, and ignore them as if the problem doesn't exist. Some people may sit on the fence, or leave things to someone else to sort out; but not dealing with conflict often means all communication stops until the conflict is addressed, or resolved. When it is ignored and we deny our part, outer conflict can harm others.

Also, when we get involved in blame, resentment and projection, it can cause relationships to drift, which causes more resentment. When we judge, separation and conflict may occur. When we choose to blame someone else for our problems, we're dealing with conflict within ourselves that we've never dealt with.

Sadly, emotional conflicts and resentments rarely have anything to do with the present moment. The present moment is usually the catalyst for buried issues to surface. Most conflicts and negativity come from past issues not addressed.

TALKING ABOUT MENTAL HEALTH

'Time to Talk Day' encourages us to talk about things like mental health. Mental health problems affect one in four of us, and yet people are still afraid to open up and talk about how they feel.

Talking about mental health helps bring people together, helps improve relationships, helps break down stereotypes; it also helps us work through a recovery process.

Talking helps take away the stigma associated with mental health, anxiety and depression. We don't have to be experts to talk, we just have to want to open up, and talk about what matters to us.

Let's talk about the things we have concerns over, the things we care about. It is important we get our thoughts and feelings out. It's time to talk about mental health.

Mental health problems can mean we struggle with talking, and not being able to talk means we may struggle with communication and relationships. Not talking may also make us more susceptible to illness, so we need to avoid this.

Since 'Time to Talk Day' was first launched in 2014, it has sparked millions of conversations in homes, in the media, online, in schools and in workplaces. It is the perfect opportunity for us to talk about things. (Source: https://www.time-to-change.org.uk)

Getting something off your chest and saying how you feel can be invigorating. It can make you feel better about what you deal with. It can also be the difference between being calm, and dealing with anxiety, or depression. Expressing how we feel is important.

ANGER AND IRRITABILITY

We sometimes have a tendency to blurt things out, but how many of us consciously connect with the fact that what we're blurting out are critical undertones, brought about through anger and irritability?

Critical undertones imply there is something lurking, something in our past that we've experienced, but we haven't yet resolved. Being angry and irritable relate to experiences we're not always consciously aware exist, but it is plausible that disorders such as anxiety and depression exist through being angry and irritable.

It is not that we actively choose to be angry and irritable, but a subliminal undertone that isn't empathetic, patient or tolerant means we're not coping with certain aspects of our lives. Disorders can emerge through anger and irritability.

It is important that when part of us loses the ability to rationalise, or we become irritated at certain issues that we're struggling with, we stand back and think about why we're feeling that way.

It is inevitable that we have stress and may struggle from time to time; what matters is how we deal with it. Unconscious thoughts are almost always at the core of our emotions and outward behaviour; and feeling angry and irritable are all signs that we're struggling with our unconscious thoughts.

To heal, we need to dig deep and deal with why we are feeling angry and irritable.

BITTERNESS

Injustice can make us feel bitter, and unless we deal with and move on from that feeling, it can turn into anger.

We may dwell on feeling bitter. It can be worse than

anger, because psychologically, bitterness can eat away at us. We need to be able to move past it, and see beyond the bitterness. Try to stand back, evaluate your circumstances and work out why you're feeling bitter and why you may be feeling so detached. Not everything you feel is about you. Decide how best to handle yourself and your situation.

Whilst we can't turn back the clock on our circumstances or our experiences, we can change the way we see them. Bitterness not only eats away at us, but may also cause symptoms of trauma, low self-confidence and irritability.

To move away from bitterness, always look at your experiences, your life and the bigger picture, and don't be distracted by the minor details. A good affirmation to remember is: *'Being positive is my choice, I shall choose to be positive.'*

OTHER PEOPLE'S EMOTIONS

Negative emotions we carry from other people are energies that, if left, can potentially become our negative emotions too.

Because our brains are like emotional sponges, it is even more important we challenge ourselves so we're not constantly being drawn into other people's emotions, particularly if their emotions are negative.

These suggestions are worth considering:

- Others aren't always the source of your negativity, so

try to work out why you're feeling negative. Dig deep, the answers are always there

- Certain situations can be difficult. Remember to take a mental break for ten to fifteen minutes, whilst you focus on your breathing and yourself
- Think about the way you respond to other people. You're not responsible for others, but you are responsible for the way you react
- You are responsible for your own perceptions and attitude

Some of us may be more susceptible to other people's negative emotions, particularly those who already have a predisposition to negative thoughts through anxiety or depression.

If you are dealing with anxiety or depression, it is even more important you're not around negative people.

CALL A SPADE A SPADE

As a child, I wanted to talk about how I felt; now I see talking as a necessity. I call a spade a spade. I describe things as they are. For me, all scenarios are black or white, there are no grey areas.

How we see things is important, but how we express ourselves is even more important. Through necessity, I have learned to speak my own truth and although my approach is straightforward and honest, my version is more palatable. While my life experiences have mostly been negative, I choose not to see or live my life that way.

Having faced my own experiences and emotional struggles over the years, I believe we should all want to face our struggles, as part of us aiming to live a more peaceful life.

How we speak our truth matters. It is part of the spiritual and healing process. We can still be truthful, candid and direct without being outspoken, rude or impolite. Unfortunately, many of us may not always strike the right balance. Instead, we may be outspoken to the point of being frank, blunt and rude.

That all depends on where we are in our own personal headspace. As we go about our lives, we may often mirror outwardly what we feel inside. When confronted by someone who is on the receiving end of how we feel, instead of being honest, we may refute it and march it straight back.

HOLDING ON TO HOPE

There's something inside of us that holds on to hope, as if our lives depend on it. Hope is an inner feeling that stays with us. It's a shining light not yet shone, a desire that something positive will happen, or if we need something to change that something will change. Hope is a place where calm resides; where serenity, knowing and wisdom blend together, hope sits and waits in the wings.

As we journey through life, we continue to hold on to hope that somehow our lives will work out and that we will feel better. Hope is a desire to live positively, a belief that our luck will change.

Hope is an unconscious expectation that things will work out. When blended with anticipation, it is a yearning that our lives will be different. Hope is our motivator. It keeps us moving, it's hope after all!

Hope is different to each of us. It is an anchor in times of uncertainty. Hope is what drives us, it's that little voice inside telling us one more time that it's not time to give up.

QUESTIONING OUR BAGGAGE

To discover the root cause of what we're dealing with requires honest introspection. Not knowing what the root causes are steals our energy from the many positive influences we may then fail to recognise.

The build-up of what we carry or deal with may lie heavily sometimes. Over time, the weight of our baggage, responsibilities, grudges and regrets may not only begin to affect our emotional health, but our physical health too.

Emotional baggage is the feelings you have from your past that you're struggling to let go of, brought about through guilt and decisions other people have made for you, and because you had no choice at the time.

Introspection is often necessary and something we can all do. When emotional baggage begins to present itself in physical ailments like backache, headaches, feeling tired and being rundown, not many of us make the connection that our baggage has anything to do with our physical health.

A headache may seem like a headache, but it's often an issue waiting to be resolved. Not learning to use introspection, deal with, or be honest with ourselves, may contribute to suppressed emotions and illness. We should learn to introspect, it helps with the 'healing and spiritual' process.

UNDERSTANDING STRESS

If we fail to recognise the signs of stress, those close to us may be on the receiving end of the symptoms of our stress.

Some stress can be good for us because it keeps us alert; there are cases where it can make us aware of danger signs and how best to avoid them, but too much can make us ill.

Living with stress without any relief can lead to 'negative stress reactions'. It is known to disturb the internal balance that can lead to physical symptoms, if it persists. Those symptoms can include the usual problems such as headaches, high blood pressure, insomnia and stomach aches.

Stress can also lead to emotional problems such as anxiety and depression. It can also hasten other symptoms and increase the risk of illness. But as long as we know and understand why we have stress, we can turn those situations around.

By us changing the way we think about things, by us being more proactive, by us dealing with our issues and us simplifying our lifestyles, we can help put a lid on stress.

THE 'WRITE AND BURN' LETTER

Not everyone will have the opportunity to speak to their parents about unresolved childhood issues that have affected them. I would always recommend children speak to their parents about events from their childhood, it's usually the best way. It's important children are able to get their message across, in a way that allows them to get the best outcome.

When parents get things wrong, children can end up with a long list of wrongdoings that can make them feel vulnerable to their own shortcomings. If you can't speak to your parents because they're not approachable, or you know they won't accept what you want to say, you can physically write 'a law of attraction letter' to them instead. It's a letter you can burn, once it has been written.

Before you start writing your letter, first unconsciously acknowledge your intentions so that the universe understands why you feel what you feel. Be willing to accept, acknowledge, and be conciliatory in your approach, so those you are writing to are clear and aware of how you feel.

Writing your 'write and burn' letter is a good opportunity for you to say exactly how you feel, so you reduce the stress you carry. Allow yourself the complete freedom to write whatever comes into your head, so that it's your letter, in your own words.

As everything and everyone is connected via their energy through the universe, when you write and then burn your letter, not only are you healing yourself, but your letter will be dispersed into the universe and its contents directed to the person you've written it to, whether they are alive or not.

The point of the exercise is to speak from the heart so that the person you're writing to understands your sentiments. Write your letter as if you're telling a story. Put down everything you feel. By sending a wish to the universe and writing your letter in this way, you release yourself from the negativity of the situation and the burden of carrying the issue.

It is a way of speaking to someone without them being in front of you, releasing yourself from any emotional ties. For the process to work you need to remain open-minded.

THE BURNING CEREMONY

As you begin to burn your letter, say, 'In the name of… (I usually say mine in the name of Buddha) I now release, burn and clear all of the negativity in my letter. I bind my letter to the light for the greater good of the universe.'

Then scatter the charred letter 'into the universe'. From my own personal experiences over the years, I find it works.

MIRRORING INTERNAL THOUGHTS

Unhappy people may often reflect their inward thoughts outwardly. They hold on to grudges as if their lives depend on it, afraid to let go, because letting go means having to face a new life. It's not how they want to live, but getting to their new life seems too difficult.

Our internal thoughts may sometimes imprison us. We know it's not how we want to feel, and we know it's not right, but it's something we often find difficult to change. It's also not unique, in fact it's not unique at all. We've probably all done it. Outwardly, as we continue to reflect our unconscious thoughts, we do so without question, even though we know our behaviour may hurt us and those we love.

We need to understand that our outward behaviour is simply a reflection of our internal thoughts and these can always be changed. A change in mindset is a positive change for new opportunities. If we see change as something negative, our external behaviour reflects our internal negative thinking, so we should avoid this.

People may feel more comfortable when they understand that change is a time for new opportunities. An appetite for change can always be developed, even if it's not always there from the start. It's all about mindset and a mindset can always be changed.

CONFLICT AND LEARNING

Whilst conflict is inevitable and can be part of everyday life, it can also be difficult to move away from it. We can always use our experiences involving conflict to embrace new understanding.

Conflict is a way of telling us that something isn't right, that perhaps we've said or done something that reflects an uncertain outcome. Conflict is something to be dealt with, a new way of responding to a person, or situation. It is an opportunity for us to learn, an opportunity for us to question the way we do things.

Understanding that what we are doing isn't working properly should prompt us to think differently. We should stop retaliating because that is what conflict is. Instead, we should learn to consider our actions more purposefully, so that we may create more conciliatory choices. There is always more than one response open to us.

When we create a sense of control and balance, and choose a better way to think, we lose the fear, frustration, and isolation we associate with being a victim. We don't have to be victims; we are only as much a victim as we choose to be.

We can choose to walk away from a life that involves conflict. It is about changing our perceptions. We can choose not to see people as perpetrators, and instead, use mediation as a tool to communicate, to get our point across.

When we use conflict destructively, there are no winners. It's not a competition and yet we often behave as if we are in competition with each other, needing to have the last word. Conflict has little to do with argument, what the other person said, or what we said.

Conflict is something that's inside of us, usually brought about from childhood experiences, not yet dealt with. Conflict is the scapegoat of all our problems.

ACKNOWLEDGING EMOTIONAL PAIN

To heal emotional pain, we need to first acknowledge we have it. Where that may seem obvious to some, others are not always aware of what their emotional pain is. Outwardly, we don't always make the correlation between how we feel now and our past experiences.

But we all have varying degrees of emotional pain or trauma in our energy field. Unfortunately, when we fail to turn our attention to any type of emotional pain, we may end up in emotional conflict, which can be the difference between staying well and becoming ill. We should learn to turn our attention to it.

It is important to be aware of our emotions and bring those into our conscious thoughts, so that we can acknowledge and deal with them. We may learn from an early age not to talk about things, but unless we are encouraged to talk about how we feel, a lot of what we feel can get buried.

Harbouring any unconscious experiences from our past may come to the surface at some point. Emotions that aren't dealt with can turn into anger issues, and anger issues may inhibit spiritual and emotional healing.

LESSONS LEARNED

We learn that our most valuable lessons come through our thoughts, our emotions, our perceptions and our words.

We learn that emotions may determine a particular experience and outcome, whether that outcome is right or wrong, that we have control over some of our decisions, and we can learn and grow from those decisions, as we emotionally and spiritually grow. We also learn that through emotional hurt we can grow, we fail so that we can know success, we lose so that we can learn how to win, and that we can grow through some of our toughest challenges.

We also learn that when we think we are lost we find ourselves, and that our perceptions define an outcome. If the outcome turns out to be wrong, then that's what we should work on.

We learn that we are masters of our own destiny, that when we think there is no hope, we can still find hope; and where we are down, we can bring ourselves back up again.

LESSONS AND MISTAKES

Mistakes are a consequence of the lessons we fail to learn. We need to understand where we go wrong because, without understanding, we may go on to create more and inevitably may also come unstuck.

Understanding our lessons means cutting down on our mistakes. Lessons learned and fewer mistakes equals a happier and an easier life.

THE ART OF RESISTING

It's easy to resist the very things that can help us grow. Instead, we control and box in the things we don't want to deal with, in the hope that those things stay boxed. For some of us, it's almost become an art form, we do it so well.

We may often resist trying to control anything painful. As we start to exhibit signs of anxiety from this resistance, we continue to ignore the signs, and may fail to consciously pay attention to them.

The irony is that the more we push and bury our issues underground, the more we will be forced to deal with them. We resist until we can resist no more. We do this because we're afraid to deal with the inevitable. We resist because we're afraid to face our fears, we're afraid of any potential conflict, and we're afraid to let go. Ironically, the more we resist, the more frequent those things become. Issues don't go away until we deal with them.

Resistance is part of our false sense of reality. Most things seem out of our reach until we bring them back; we resist, we shy away from the very things we need to deal with.

When we choose this path, we choose not to come to terms with things. We resist because we've already told ourselves that what we're trying to achieve is totally out of reach, and that's simply not true.

LEARNING TO COMPROMISE

We all want our relationships to run smoothly. We may expect and want others to compromise and yet we don't always compromise ourselves, with some of us choosing not to compromise at all. Being open allows us to be honest in what we're asking and what we're expecting back from others.

The dynamics of our relationships are very much the catalyst for how we choose to communicate and interact with others. From around the age of seven those patterns are already formed. Our upbringing, our environment, the family dynamics, everything we emotionally deal with, play a part in how we may choose to interact and whether we will compromise. Being open helps us with this. If we are open as children, we should be more compromising as adults. (Source: https://news.softpedia.com)

Although relationships should be based on compromise, we should never compromise on bad behaviour. By bad behaviour, I mean living without integrity or a moral compass, using sarcasm or the ego as a communication tool, not being honest, and using words that belittle, or set out to hurt others.

We should all want to communicate with truth, integrity, decency, and sincerity. When we learn to incorporate these things into our lives, there's no reason for us not to want to compromise.

ATTITUDE

The older we are, the more likely we are to want to understand the impact of our attitude. Although we may remember certain events, it is our attitude pertaining to those events that define how others remember us.

Our education, experiences, past and life in general are all important, but our attitude to those things is more important, because without the right attitude we may struggle to move forward with our lives. Also, without having the right attitude, people may go on to form the wrong opinions of us.

But we are free to choose how we respond to others, in the same way others are free to choose how they respond to us. If through our attitude we show empathy and compassion, others should want to react towards us in the same way.

If we believe in spirituality, and we get back what we hand out, our attiude and how we react is going to be an important element of this.

DETERMINING OUR EXPERIENCES

The way we look at life determines our thoughts and experiences and we are responsible for both. We should first cut through the belief systems we create for ourselves, so we're looking at the bigger picture. The bigger picture presents us with an opportunity to change the way we see the world.

Also, if we fail to explore the possibilities that lie beyond our conscious thoughts, we may block finding the answers to some of our issues. The limits we have are the ones we create and place on ourselves. We may look at events and situations, and interpret other people's thoughts and feelings through our own set of beliefs. Our beliefs include past experiences, culture, values and faith that help us to form our beliefs about ourselves and other people.

That's fine, but it can also mean we get stuck, if the meaning we give to events is based upon other people's values, rather than our own. If that is the case, our values and beliefs may be other people's, not what we want for ourselves, and these may determine our experiences. Our experiences need to be based on our own wants and needs and not what others want for us, or have taught us to think.

Growing up, we may not always be taught to think for ourselves, instead we may be taught to follow family values that won't necessarily incorporate spiritual concepts, and what life really means.

MEDITATION BENEFITS

The physical, spiritual and emotional benefits of meditation have been acknowledged for thousands of years. Scientists, spiritualists, philosophers and religious leaders have heralded the power of meditation, by witnessing awareness.

Known as deep reflection, mindfulness, or contemplation, meditation allows us to drift into the space between our thoughts. Because meditation works on a subconscious level, if we do it for long enough, it begins to express itself through the subtle choices we go on to make. The more we meditate, the more conscious our thoughts, decisions and daily actions become.

Meditation helps us achieve a greater alignment between what we think, what we say and how we behave. It allows us to slow down, when the world turns at a faster pace. Meditation helps us re-evaluate how we live and what is important to us.

Meditation gives us a deeper sense of calm, it helps us manage a broader perspective on our issues and therefore greater clarity, allowing us to channel grace and tap into our more authentic self. The emotional shift of meditation can be so subtle, that we may not even see these meditation benefits straight away.

If continued over a period of weeks, or months, we can begin to acquire a deeper understanding of ourselves and how a spiritual path might work, a path where we'll make new discoveries about ourselves that we never even knew existed.

FINDING OUR OWN WAY

How many of us spend our lives living someone else's life? Living with dreams and goals that are not ours, or will never be achieved, but instead basing our lives on what other people expect, or want for us.

It is human nature for us to make comparisons, but that can make us feel worse. When we perceive other people to be better, or more successful than we are, we may start to make comparisons. Instead, we should understand our own qualities and pay attention to ourselves. We may never know what we're capable of, if we continue to compare ourselves, or follow other people's values and beliefs.

We are all individuals with unique personalities. We should get to know everything about ourselves that makes us unique, not rely on others, and find our own way.

USING EMPATHY AND SYMPATHY

Empathy and sympathy are closely related, but have different meanings. Empathy is feeling what someone else feels, while sympathy is about action. When you meet someone with empathy it wouldn't be difficult to see, they are sympathetic too.

Someone who is sympathetic but not empathetic may fail to connect emotionally with anyone. Words express thoughts, but it is us acting on words that show we care. 'Actions speak louder than words'; it is not enough to just say, we need to act on what we say. While having sympathy is important, having empathy is the glue that holds our relationships together.

A little more about empathy:

- Empathy helps us connect emotionally with others. Emotionally we may begin to feel less alone, but we need to also make the effort to open up
- Empathy helps us heal. When someone shows they care, it helps us see that we can care back
- Empathy brings people and families closer together. Empathy enables us to understand first-hand what someone feels
- Empathy brings trust
- Empathy promotes spiritual and emotional healing

Empathy is also the building block to relationships and that's what relationships need to thrive on. Everyone may sympathise but not everyone can empathise.

DEALING WITH FAILURE

Life can be full of new opportunities. When one door closes another door opens, and we should make ourselves aware of those opportunities.

None of us will have control all the time because it's unrealistic, but we can have it often. For example, we have control over the things we perceive, the things we fail at and how we choose to come through the other end.

Failing means we have lost sight of how to reach our potential. It isn't necessarily bad, but at the time it can seem like the end of the world. Failing is an opportunity to reflect, to learn new things, to open new doors. It is also an opportunity to find a resolve, and for us to make the necessary changes.

Failing gives us the opportunity to stand back, to start anew, to find a level of acceptance on why we may have failed. If I fail at something, it's my responsibility. If I fail because someone else was responsible for my decision, it is still up to me to find a way through.

It is okay to fail. Life teaches us that failing is one of our most valuable tools, but we need to be prepared to learn our lessons and understand the reasons why we failed.

ADVERSITY AND RESILIENCE

We can start to build on our resilience through adversity. Challenges and difficulties that we've had to confront and overcome can serve to strengthen our confidence, strength of character, and our ability to conquer future adversities.

When we respond positively to some of our biggest challenges, we can find the emotional strength, perseverance, and courage to dig deep. Although adversity challenges us in different ways, it is our ability to endure and bounce back from our struggles that creates emotional resilience, so that we are able to move forward with our lives.

LEARNING TO LIKE OURSELVES

Do we really like ourselves and, if we don't, how then can we be honest with ourselves? The more we like who we are, the more honest we will be, with ourselves and others.

We should be open, kind and gentle on ourselves. We need to look at all aspects of ourselves, what we want to improve, the parts of our lives we're not happy with and the parts of our lives that are a challenge; the parts we need to change.

Perhaps we need to go back to basics, back to the beginning, how we got to this place, where it all started, through our childhood, what makes us, because this is the basis upon which foundations are built. Without strong foundations in place, we may struggle to like ourselves, struggle to live well, or at least spiritually well.

At the same time, we should look at our aspirations, our goals, our career, the people we're in contact with, anything we need to improve on and change for the better.

NEGATIVE TO POSITIVE

We can change our perceptions from negative to positive; we can choose to focus our perceptions on the positive. We can choose to look at a situation and see the good, or we can choose to look at the same situation and see the bad. We can always choose to perceive our lives differently.

Most of us rely on our unconscious, the part of the

mind that occurs automatically, that's not readily available for introspection, instead of using our perceptions to change and create the lives we want.

Also, we should learn to look at our lives, so that our thoughts aren't being filtered through our unconscious all the time, and instead learn to live presently.

SIGNS OF PERSONAL GROWTH

When someone is at one with themselves, they feel happy and whole, and are in sync with their lives. They don't take offence, and are not easily wounded or triggered by other people's words, or actions. They also don't take things personally and can quite often see the bigger picture.

Those who haven't gone through the healing process may be jealous or annoyed at those who have; but even where there may be conflict, there are still opportunities for self-healing. It is important we acknowledge our feelings and underlying pain. It is also important we recognise deep wounds that are being brought to the surface; process and address those and any past issues, so that they can be worked through.

We all have our own journey, we all have issues and we all have lessons. Ask yourself what you're being taught and work on seeing how your issues and any disputes can be resolved in an amicable, non-judgmental way.

When people take responsibility and control for their lives, they begin to see the hidden gifts being offered, the learning; the lessons and the personal growth. The very things that allow them to grow, heal and renew.

NOTHING TO FIX

I came to the conclusion a long time ago that we don't have to be fixed to be healed, instead we should be flexible enough to be ready for what life throws at us.

Living with a disability and having faced many challenges, I don't see myself as broken, my disabilities are just something I was born with. I guess it all depends on how we see ourselves.

Having certain beliefs doesn't take away our pain, but as long as we're open-minded, understanding our beliefs can help alleviate stress. We're spiritual beings, having a human experience, and that means we will always have certain challenges along the way.

Being fixed isn't about acquiring perfection. We can heal without being fixed or acquiring perfection. It is about us having the ability and willingness to accept ourselves unconditionally that allows for emotional and spiritual growth and healing. It is all to do with the mindset and how we see ourselves.

When we live with acceptance and are able to emotionally heal, there will be nothing for us to physically fix. We may struggle in our everyday lives and still see ourselves and our lives positively.

HOW TO FEEL HAPPY

There is often a misconception about being happy. Being happy is a soulful journey that starts from the soul. Being happy isn't about making other people happy. Instead, we should understand ourselves, our experiences, our baggage, our dissapointments, our lives, as well as our trials and triumphs.

Learn to love who you are and what you become, because that is where the power is and where happiness starts. What we add from there, continues to add to how we feel about ourselves.

MY LESSONS AND EXPERIENCES

Looking back on my life, if I had my time again, I would keep my lessons and change my experiences. I am sure about that.

I've heard it said many times that we choose the life we come into. I would have chosen some, but not all of my experiences. I would have wanted a life less difficult. If I could have learned my lessons without having lived traumatic experiences, then that would have been my choice.

My spiritual beliefs have been instrumental in helping me understand my lessons, to live my life with purpose, and a certain ease. Whilst my experiences have shown me many lessons, I would have preferred those lessons to come in from less harsh avenues.

Over the years, and through my writing, my spiritual beliefs have paved the way for me to do what I do.

DETACHING ONESELF

When we begin not to care and consciously take our emotions away from thinking about a particular person or issue, we take away the element of struggle. The reason we struggle is because we continue to carry the emotions that attach us to a particular person, or issue.

When we stop caring, we take away the stress, and give ourselves the ammunition to address what we have failed to deal with, or whatever we happen to be dealing with at the time.

The healing and spiritual process can only begin when we learn to emotionally detach, and in some cases physically detach, if that's what we feel we need to do.

HANDLING BAD NEWS

The right attitude and focus helps pave the way for positive thinking in difficult circumstances. Being positive is an important response for bad news, but it is not something that happens spontaneously. We have to continue to work at it.

No one gets to change bad news or the outcome, but it helps the healing process if we are able to react to it in a positive way. Being calm and proactive allows us to take bad news in our stride, but it needs to be honed. It's not easy, but it becomes easier if we learn to deal with it in childhood.

The first time I had to cope with bad news was in my early twenties when my grandmother passed away. Now my spiritual beliefs help me handle bad news.

Bad news invokes an emotional response, as much as good news. It is a part of life that is necessary, in some cases even more. We learn more about ourselves when we have to deal with bad news.

It's not something I did as a child; but now when I am faced with bad news, I ask myself questions so that I can work through handling it. Questions like what may have caused the bad event to happen? Why did it happen, why was it allowed to happen and how could something like that be avoided next time? Did the problem happen because of a health issue that hadn't been addressed?

Asking questions helps us to see the bigger picture and can often make hearing bad news less scary. There is always a reason behind why something bad happens and we need to understand why. Once we have understanding, it becomes part of the healing process.

TRYING TO BE BETTER

If you believe in spirituality, you'll know how important it is to try to do better than you did yesterday, to be a better person.

We may not always think about others, we may not do right by others, and we may hurt others because we're unconsciously hurting too, but that is no excuse. Trying to be better means we take out certain traits like self-righteousness, and the ego. It is a goal we should never lose sight of.

Through spirituality, we can change to be more considerate of others, be more tolerant, learn to embrace others. Through spirituality, we can start to appreciate the little things. The little things help us to stay grounded and humble; it means we are able to focus our attention on what heals us, nurtures and sustains us.

Although being spiritual cannot stop the bad things from happening, by trying to be better people, we can learn how to handle ourselves better and that helps us in our personal lives, in our relationships.

By practising gratitude, and challenging ourselves to think positively, we're shifting the emphasis, and that can help us find a valuable source of mental balance. It's something we should all try to do.

HEALING THROUGH REFLECTION

Reflection is a process that helps to create an internal space for exploring traumatic experiences that have hurt and continue to hurt us. Reflection works better when we practise it on our own, and is a good way for us to explore our internal dialogue.

Reflection is also a good way for us to explore our differences in a group situation. It allows others to mediate with us, to say what they feel, for us to listen and for them to then listen to us.

Reflection also helps us study our feelings in depth so that we come away with a more positive understanding of ourselves, other people's perspectives and our situation.

Reasons for using reflection:

- It helps us identify and learn from our mistakes
- When we've mastered it for ourselves, we can help others
- It gives us a clear perspective
- It makes us happier
- Through a clearer perspective we can work on change

It is easy for us to say we want to heal, but unless we are prepared to put in the hard work, we may never heal. Reflection is a good way to bring a close to many past issues often left unresolved.

IMPROVING OUR CONFIDENCE

How do we improve our confidence? How do we turn our lives around from having no confidence to having little confidence? These suggestions are a good place to start.

Learn to be kind and generous: when you're kind and generous, you not only improve how you see yourself, but you learn to treat others as you would want them to treat you. This leads to a happier life.

Improve your self-image and how you want others to see you: when you take good care of yourself, you improve your self-image and that makes you feel good about yourself. When you feel good about yourself, you start to believe in yourself more. When you begin to believe in yourself, you start to believe you can do the things you've always thought you couldn't, and your confidence starts to increase.

Increasing your competence increases your confidence: but you have to give it a go. Without having a go, or at least trying things, you may never have the confidence, or feel you're competent enough. It's the act of trying a new skill or experience that increases your competence, which increases your confidence. It can be a vicious circle, but it is important to get past that if you are to succeed.

Know and live by your principles: what are the principles upon which your life is measured? The majority of us go through life without any understanding of what our moral compass is and what that means, and without knowing, our lives may continue to be difficult and directionless.

Our moral compass should be based on the 'golden rules' and 'morality' that leads us to live a more spiritual life. Perhaps start with the principle of 'do unto others as you would have them do unto you'. The golden rule, which is at the core of morality, should be used by each of us, so that we are able to create a better, kinder society for ourselves and future generations to come.

Simplify your life: so that you exclude the people who

don't have your back and you know are holding you back; because those people may pull you back even further. Also, learn not to look over your shoulder at what others have, and try not to criticise other people. The more you criticise other people, the more negativity you'll have to deal with. That can knock your confidence.

Learn to go with the flow: accept what you can't change and change what you can, as you continue to move forward.

Although confidence grows and comes with maturity, as we face daily issues, it's easy for the confidence we have to get knocked. When we start to believe in ourselves, we can begin to live with, and increase our confidence.

TAKE OUT THE WORRY

We may never have peace of mind when we're too concerned with what other people think.

When we worry and have little self-confidence and struggle to focus on what's ahead, we can mentally and emotionally struggle. When we lose sight of what is important, we may sometimes let stress in. However, when we can begin to understand the bigger picture and we are able to take out the worry; when we understand that it doesn't matter what other people think, and when we begin to learn what is important, we can begin to have peace.

Although realistically there may never be a time when we are completely free of worry or stress, working on removing some of our issues can help bring more peace.

ENERGETIC HEALING

Energy healing is an aspect of complementary and alternative medicine.

The energy field known as the 'aura' comprises a number of layers that not only surround us, but spread or flow throughout our cells and bodies.

The mind is made up of two parts, the conscious part, the part that in computer terms is the 'hardware', and the aura, which is the 'software'. They work together. The aura stores our memories, everything that has ever happened to us, not just on this plane but long before we enter our physical bodies. The different layers of the aura have a different purpose.

It is also responsible for our immune system. Disturbances of the Integrated Energy Fields and Internal Energy Fields are a precursor to illness and disease and problems with our mental, emotional and physical well-being. Therefore, how the aura functions is vital for good health and well-being.

Trauma, mental and emotional stress, physical distress, false belief systems and environmental stress, are blocks that can interfere with our personal growth. If left, they can become stored in our energy fields, impacting our ability to function at optimum level, and as a result we may fail to reach our full potential. (Source: https://www. healingenergy.com.au)

Energetic healing allows for the healing process to begin, by repairing, rebalancing and clearing blocks in our energy fields, so that our bodies can realign and rebalance. Energetic healing can also identify issues before they manifest as pain in the physical body. It alerts us to our consciousness, to the areas we need to work on, so that we can heal, rebalance and maintain health, vitality and harmony.

FORMS OF ENERGETIC HEALING

Energetic healing manipulates our body's energy circuits to help regain balance, and bring about our body's own natural healing mechanisms.

Therapies that incorporate energetic healing include reiki, reflexology and acupuncture. Energetic healing also encompasses lesser known therapies including aura and chakra balancing: flower and vibrational essences, crystal healing, spiritual healing, and colour therapy.

Practitioners are usually trained in a number of different therapies and combine these therapies in their own unique way. Many also combine intuitive skills with their practical and theoretical skills. (Source: http://www.healingenergy. com.au)

Energetic healing is a holistic approach that looks beyond the physical, to help balance the chakras, meridians, nari and auric bodies, to where the cause of the disease or disorder can be located.

RID YOURSELF OF CLUTTER

We can spend a lifetime accumulating 'material clutter', and can also accumulate worry, negative self-talk and guilt, also known as 'mental clutter'.

All these things can become distractions, which can make us physically sick. When we learn to let go of the mental clutter, we can put new practices in place that can help us be more positive, as well as helping us stay well in the process.

Sadly, it doesn't stop there. When we carry mental clutter, we may also begin to bring in material clutter. But when we are able to let go of mental clutter, we may also decide to let go of material clutter. It's beneficial to our mental and emotional health to let go of unnecessary material things.

We should also learn to say 'no' without feeling guilty, to let go of having to do things perfectly, to deal with negativity and focus on inner healing and positivity. We should also learn to deal with issues, before they escalate into something bigger.

We should spend more time with people who lift and support us, while we continue to work on inner peace. When we learn to simplify our lives and are able to reduce the material clutter, we can work towards finding inner peace.

BEING INVISIBLE

Being invisible usually happens because of an undercurrent, a disparity between how we feel and how something is. Emotionally, it's easy to feel distant and feeling invisible is a consequence of this. Being invisible is all about what's going on internally, how we feel about ourselves and how we choose what we present to the world.

Being invisible means emotionally and mentally withdrawing, so you're choosing not to draw attention to yourself, choosing to back off, or stay away. It means not talking so you don't draw attention to yourself, averting your gaze, or looking down to avoid eye contact; avoiding situations so you don't have to face people. That said, you can still be physically present and be mentally invisible.

It is not something others may comprehend or understand, but we know it exists. For those people with little understanding, it may even be dismissed, minimised or ignored. Being invisible to the world is only something we notice.

Also, being invisible has nothing to do with how we look to another person or our presence, it's about our worth, self-esteem, confidence and how little we feel we can physically and emotionally present ourselves to the world. It is a coping mechanism, one that keeps us safe.

It's a hideout, a space we occupy until such time we feel strong enough to get back into our lives. It feels normal and, for all intents and purposes, it is normal. It's something we come to accept as the norm, but it's also something we can change at any time.

Being invisible means there is no right or wrong way for us to feel, it is whatever we have to deal with at the time. Being invisible means we have somewhere in our mind to go when things don't feel right. It is our retreat. It allows us to tap into our emotions, so that we can explore our thoughts and feelings; it helps us cope.

Being invisible doesn't mean we have to sacrifice ourselves individually, it simply means not having to be assertive all the time, and choosing when we fit in. Choosing when we fit in may begin to reflect a deeper sense of our self-confidence, than us having to stand out.

HOW THE EMOTIONS WORK

The psyche is responsible for our emotions, thoughts and behaviour. It is the totality of the human mind, unconscious and conscious. It controls our response patterns to our environment and recreates our unconscious experiences, which reside below our level of conscious thinking.

As adults we may spend time observing our emotions. It is a way for us to understand our lives, to understand we don't need to copy other people's emotional behaviour and, in some cases, for us to right a wrong.

Once we are able to analyse and recognise character trait patterns that reside below our level of conscious awareness, we can begin the healing process. Trauma stems from patterns that continually play out on a conscious level, but they reside in our unconscious thinking. For us to gain access to our unconscious thinking, we need to engage our intuition. It is only when we are able to change our unconscious thinking that we can change our conscious thinking and behaviour patterns.

It is easy for us to see this when children engage in role play. Have you ever noticed how children enact traumatic events they've seen over and over, without being aware of why they're doing it? For example, children playing rough with their dolls and then kissing them better. In adults, it is our inner child that re-enacts our traumas from childhood, until we are able to solve them and find different conclusions.

The reality is that many of us may never go on to recognise trauma in this way and, if we do, we may choose to ignore the associated trauma behaviour patterns, because they're too difficult to deal with.

LEARNING TO LISTEN

We tend to listen on our own terms. We listen, not to understand or to hear, but to jump at the opportunity for us to speak again, whether that means agreeing to what's being said, or simply putting in our penny's worth.

We take conversations the way we want them to go. It's all about us. It may be better to think about our connections, how we may superficially listen and how we may superficially connect. When we speak, there's an element of us wanting to be heard, for others to admire what we say, as much as we crave appreciation and admiration for ourselves.

There is a part of us that wants to inspire. Perhaps it's because growing up we struggled to get ourselves heard; perhaps no one listened and now we want, or expect others to listen to us. Perhaps we struggled with confidence issues, and now with this new-found confidence we want others to take notice; maybe it matters to us what other people think.

Perhaps we want to be accepted, we want validation of our thoughts, perhaps we never had that as a child, and we crave it now. There may be many reasons why, but the biggest reason we need to listen is that we can never be close to anyone without connecting on a soulful level.

We need to work from a soulful level, because not doing so means we may fail to deeply connect, or bring any real purpose to our life, or our relationships.

EMOTIONAL TRAUMA

A child who witnesses or experiences emotional or physical abuse, or neglect, can often show signs of emotional trauma as an adult. A child dealing with any type of trauma will have been deeply affected.

Children may start to evaluate what everything means by the events they witness and may create an internal map of how their world looks to them. If a child has love and support, their internal map should look and feel normal.

For any child, it is important they are able to change their internal map as they grow, so that by the time they become an adult, they have created a new internal map. The old ways of interpreting the world, if it's not recorded properly, can damage the way children emotionally function as adults, and that's not easily changed.

Children who have suffered emotional trauma may create a version of themselves they think their family will love and accept. They become the person their family wants them to be. That way, they don't have to think or change anything. Those children may continue to bury how they feel, just so their needs are met.

In these circumstances, instead of children thinking about their own needs or what their needs are, they may continue to concentrate on other people's needs, aiming to please, just so they will be accepted. Where they fail to acknowledge or connect emotionally, it's not something they may consciously recognise.

But when anyone buries their emotions, they lose touch with reality, and of who they really are. It's important to challenge yourself so you can begin to connect in a way that makes you feel normal, safe and whole. If you're not connecting with your feelings, it is important you are able to challenge yourself.

A positive affirmation to use would be: *'I shall take small but significant steps.'*

WHY THINGS HAPPEN

I believe that no matter the situation, things happen for a reason and something of value can come out of it, as long as we look for the understanding. In life, there will always be valuable lessons for us to learn.

Sometimes opportunities come out of difficult situations and those opportunities show us why things happen a certain way. When I can equate and understand why things happen, I find it easier to change my perceptions and attitude.

Knowing the reason why something happens saves us from feeling we're to blame. There will always be a reason, even if it isn't what we were expecting, or one that we initially understand.

No one is free of their karmic debt, we are all accountable for our actions. When someone hurts us, the universe will want to put that right. When something bad happens, there is a lesson to learn, a reason why. Lessons encourage healing.

OVERCOMING MENTAL BLOCKS

We all have mental blocks where we're stuck and have no control over our thinking. It is like we've forgotten our thought process.

When we understand that we don't have to fit into other people's thinking, or their lives, we can overcome mental blocks. We create mental blocks when we continually believe what others think without thinking for ourselves. But believing what others think may not only leave us with an unquestioning consensus, it can also go on to inhibit our natural creative abilities; in other words, we lose our ability to think for ourselves.

Whether we're trying to solve an issue, or look at ways to change an outcome, our creative thinking is crucial to that process. To begin the process, we should first change our perspective so we're looking at the outcome differently.

We need to create how we want things to be, by accepting them as they are and not how we would like them to be. When it comes to mental blocks and creativity, it's not always a matter of looking for ways to inspire creativity, we need to understand the truth and make decisions based on our own truth, so we can overcome the mental blocks.

Truth lends itself to creativity and being able to overcome mental blocks. It is important we work on truth.

SUFFERING IN SILENCE

Suffering is based on mental and/or physical pain and can be mild, or intolerable. The intensity of our suffering also depends on the duration and frequency of its occurrence. No matter how much you're suffering, always try to let someone know how you feel.

Burying how we feel, in the hope that our suffering goes away, doesn't help. Suffering only goes away when we address the issues that are the cause of our suffering.

Through mental illness, people often suffer in silence, living secret lives around anxiety, depression and social phobias, and other debilitating psychiatric conditions. For those who struggle with talking about how they feel, they are not living their life on their own terms.

Suffering in silence can reinforce our symptoms, create a resistance and a persistant state. Suffering without finding our voice increases feelings of isolation and creates stigma, particularly if we're also dealing with a disability. It stops clearing negative thoughts and healing. It may also delay treatment and prolong suffering.

Finding our voice is the best way to work through the stigma and the best way to heal. It is important we all talk about how we feel.

CHANGING OURSELVES

Personality traits are made up of various facets. For example, it's okay for someone who is a conversationalist and easy to talk to, but what about someone who is spiteful and selfish, who avoids responsibility with a propensity for lying?

While our personalities contribute to the actions and decisions that we go on to make, it is possible for us to change certain aspects of our personality through being mindful, and changing certain beliefs, behaviour patterns and habits.

By taking steps to actively change ourselves, we become

more balanced individuals; by working on ourselves we come to understand our personality traits better, and as a result can make our journey towards self-discovery.

SENTIMENTS BEHIND THE WORDS

If we took the time to look at and understand the sentiments behind people's words, we would probably all get on better.

We can spend our lives listening to people's words, but never look behind their meaning or sentiments; what their words say, or why people say what they say. Instead, we need to understand the person and the reasoning behind their words. If more of us understood people's sentiments and why they say what they say, we probably wouldn't jump to conclusions, or have to deal with fall outs.

When we look at the sentiments behind people's words, we should see sincerity, a refined sensibility. We should also see a person's vulnerable side, where they're influenced by their emotions, rather than by fact or reason.

We may always be happy to appeal to other people's sentiments, so long as they're open, honest and transparent with us. Sentiment plays an important part in all communication; it should be the substance for all relationships, for how people communicate.

When we come to understand a person's meaning behind their words and tone, we may understand their attitude, emotions, and their opinions better. Also, when we understand the person behind the sentiment, we're less likely to jump to the wrong conclusions about them, or for them to jump to the wrong conclusions about us.

DEALING WITH GUILT

Feelings of guilt, if they are not addressed, may intensify. But dealing with guilt is not something we easily manage, or remedy.

Guilt can interfere with our thoughts and feelings. It is responsible for denial, and for harbouring resentment, particularly if the resentment is from another person's behaviour that they've made us responsible for. Over the years we can learn that it's okay to let go and that we're not always responsible for other people's behaviour.

Guilt in itself is inoffensive, it's the attachment of guilt to a particular circumstance that makes it harmful. Guilt can also lead to criticism and expressing anger at others, sometimes in circumstances where it is completely unwarranted.

Guilt may also trigger reactive behaviour, which goes against our core values. Guilt stops us from moving on, it breaks our spirit and stops healthy communication. Guilt never serves a purpose; it simply causes more stress.

We can carry guilt even though we may be unaware we're carrying it, whether we're responsible or not. If the other person doesn't take responsibility, we may own their guilt.

But without letting go of guilt and finding ways to deal

with guilt, we can emotionally alienate ourselves and live with the most miserable of existences. When we continue to carry guilt, the impact of guilt on our health can be damaging.

It is up to each of us to own what belongs to us. It is not up to us to carry other people's guilt, because they fail to accept, or apologise for what they've done.

ADMITTING OUR GUILT

There is no need for us to feel guilty, unless we've got a reason, and if we do have something to feel guilty about, then we should address it.

For those who carry guilt, or choose to live in denial over their guilt, it is important they soul search and deal with their culpability.

It is important to recognise our actions and what we've done, instead of making what we've done someone else's problem. The people we have wronged know, as does the universe. Our conscience also knows, it is not something we can easily avoid.

Also, just because we're in denial doesn't make what we have done right. These things may seem easier to ignore, but in the longer term they never are; particularly as we may have to grapple with our conscience and that never gives in, or up.

MENTAL HEALTH ISSUES

Mental health is a psychological state where we function at a satisfactory level around our emotions and behaviour. To admit we deal with issues, or recognise we have emotional issues, is the hardest thing we may ever do.

It is tragic that in the twenty-first century, we still don't openly talk about things and say how we feel. Instead we may ignore and isolate our feelings, in the hope those feelings may go away without us having to look for outside help.

There needs to be a shift in how people come to discuss their feelings. With information being more readily accessible, we can lose the stigma surrounding mental health issues. If the stigma wasn't there, more people would feel comfortable in coming forward to say how they feel. Mental health needs to stay out of the shadows, so that more people talk about how they feel, and about the issues concerning them.

When there is a purpose to our struggles, it is OK to struggle. Having a disability, I know first-hand what it feels like to struggle, and where we may be stigmatised, our struggles often may continue to go unnoticed. We need to be open and honest about mental health and we need to overcome the stigma.

Whilst mental health issues are being talked about more openly now, there still needs to be more everyday conversations, so that it's not something we shy away from. For those who may struggle to find their starting point, I find a good affirmation is *'I shall be kind and gentle to myself.'*

MEN AND MENTAL HEALTH

Mental health is something that concerns us all, but statistics show that 40% of men don't talk to anyone about their mental health.

Mental health continues to be a taboo subject for many men, who deal with feelings of sadness, anxiety and loneliness alone and in silence, but it doesn't have to be this way.

Mental health statistics and facts:

- 12.5% of men suffer from one of the common mental health disorders, such as anxiety and depression.
- 76% of suicides are committed by men. Suicide is the biggest cause of death in men under the age of thirty-five.
- 36% of psychologist referrals are for men.

This simply should not be taboo. With more people coming forward to talk about mental health and discussions around mental health being encouraged, both men and women should feel comfortable talking about how they feel. Societal gender norms and preconceptions, the media, family and environment, all still contribute to stereotyping men as strong, independent and self-confident, but it is up to us as individuals to get past that. (Source: https://www.medicalnewstoday.com)

As a society we need to break down gender roles and stereotypes. It's important we encourage each other to talk about how we feel, irrespective of gender.

There is no shame in men admitting they feel sad, or vulnerable. There is often a stigma, which can go back to childhood. But hopefully if parents encourage children to talk about their feelings, children will start to participate.

Whilst it's not easy to talk about the things we struggle with mentally, it's better than having to deal with the illness that it can subsequently cause. We may not grow up in a world where we feel free to discuss our feelings, but if we've seen our parents talk freely, we should learn to talk, and even if we haven't, we can try to adopt a more open approach for ourselves.

Men, in particular, may want to talk openly, but may feel unable to do so. Addressing gender roles and stereotypes can help encourage men to feel more comfortable discussing their feelings. Moving forward, we should all encourage and be encouraged to talk about mental health regardless of gender.

A DIP IN THE ROAD

Events beyond our control may force us to take a dip in the road. Those events may take us down a completely different path from the one we started on, or may lead us to a different decision we might not otherwise have made.

While any new road may not have been our first choice, that doesn't mean it's the wrong one. Sometimes the new road is the right choice, even though it's not what we intended or started, but it's the road we finish on.

The path of life never runs smooth, things happen to change our path, and it helps to be prepared. Even if the path we find ourselves on is not our original path, things can turn out for the best. Often, our new set of circumstances can turn out to be better than our first.

IT'S OKAY NOT TO FORGIVE

If you've experienced trauma or neglect, you may have heard someone say, you are supposed to forgive the perpetrator but you've not quite got there: there are some circumstances where it's okay not to forgive.

You may forgive because you've been guilt tripped into thinking it's the right thing to do, or you're afraid others may think you're unkind if you don't, but not forgiving someone has nothing to do with being unkind.

Not everyone who goes through trauma or neglect sees that the perpetrator deserves or needs to be forgiven, particularly if what they've done is wilful. You should go with how you feel, and not settle with something just because it makes others feel better.

When it comes to family, we may often choose to keep the peace because it's easier, but appeasing family doesn't change the deed, nor does it mend a broken relationship. When we learn to acknowledge the most negative of feelings, those feelings can become easier.

We need to recognise and understand the motives behind the deed and use them as a way to release how we feel about those who hurt us. To forgive is to excuse the deed.

Anything that's done with wilful intent can be perceived as abusive; it is our understanding of abuse that unburdens us. It is important not to feel burdened, instead we should feel empowered that we have come through the other end with an explanation of our experiences, in a way that allows us the freedom to choose whether we forgive.

We can still heal, and choose not to forgive. It is our understanding that allows us to move on, without us forgiving.

IT'S ALL IN THE TONE

We set the tone on how we live our lives through our words and actions, what we say, and how we behave. The energy we bring either moves us towards a desired outcome, or an outcome less desirable.

When we set the tone, we establish the way an activity, or event happens. We set the tone and shape what's possible. But setting a good tone means we need to learn to respect our differences and show a personal interest; to listen and learn, whilst keeping an open mind on the possibilities.

We may set the tone by correcting past experiences, asking the right questions, sharing information, openly communicating and being transparent. What we say we will do, we should do. Integrity is everything.

We may lack integrity when what we say isn't in alignment with our intentions. Our values and behaviour need to be completely in sync. We need to show others we are serious about what we want to create and what our intentions are.

We set the tone through how we describe our experiences, how we talk about ourselves. Our experiences are filled with emotion, and our words can hurt ourselves and others. We need to think about our tone and how we use our words. It is up to families to help set a positive tone.

People learn a lot about us through our tone. Our mindset and attitude are revealed through our words. Also, what we value, our doubts, concerns and worries are all revealed through our tone.

When we unconsciously continue to focus on negative experiences, we may have lost sight of how we project ourselves, but again this is still something we can fix.

WHEN WE RESPOND, AND REACT

I am sure we've all been in this situation: reacting to something someone says, instead of stepping back to think about what our reaction should be. Most of the time this won't get us into trouble.

But we need to consider the risk of what might happen if we say something without putting some thought into it, in the same way we may receive a comment that is not appropriate. No matter what's been said, try to place importance on your integrity and spirituality instead, rather than on the person making the comment towards you.

Thoughts are fleeting, but a reaction can be permanent. It is important not to react in those circumstances, our gut may always want to react, but it's important not to. When we stand back and think things through, we can achieve a better outcome.

LEARNING FROM OUR MISTAKES

Learning from our mistakes is pivotal to our success. Without our mistakes we cannot emotionally or spiritually grow, or understand what it is to succeed.

When anyone gives us feedback, we can learn from it. Feedback shouldn't be seen as a reason to think we're being criticised, or we have failed. Instead, it should be used as an opportunity to change what isn't working.

Mistakes are simply a benchmark for further investigation. Not succeeding doesn't mean we haven't been successful; it simply means we need to look at a different approach. Working through any challenge is a success, because each challenge brings us to a different place. It is all in how we choose to look at things. Not walking away with first prize doesn't mean we've failed. Finishing a challenge is success in itself.

We learn more from our mistakes than from our successes. We never stop to question success, we just take it for granted and that chapter gets closed. It's also wrong to think that because we have success in one area of our life that other areas may be just as successful.

We can learn and grow to be more successful when we work through the basics of how we got there. We need to experiment and try out new things. Being okay with criticism, however constructive, allows for potential success further down the line.

Many of us may continue to see feedback as criticism, but it should be taken as constructive. Feedback allows us to think about what we're doing; it enables us to change certain elements so that we may find success second time around.

WHEN SUPPORT WORKS

Looking at other people's lives and thinking their lives are perfect, may often make us look at our own lives and what we have. Fairy tales often portray perfection, but for many of us, our realities are very different. With the right support in place, it is possible to achieve our goals.

When we're not able to get support from others, it is important we learn to support ourselves in the form of understanding and patience.

EMOTIONS AND EXPRESSION

We all have different ways of coping and dealing with our emotions that are conditioned through our cultural experiences and upbringing, both of which play a pivotal part.

For example, people who live in Mediterranean countries may express themselves openly over losing a loved one, whereas those from Northern European countries may be encouraged, or expected to grieve by themselves so as not to offend, or cause others to feel uncomfortable.

But all emotions, negative and positive, play their part in today's world. They need to be expressed, because not expressing emotions may invite illness in.

It is the most natural thing in the world to feel anger, to be anxious and to feel sadness, in the same way it is to feel joy, excitement and contentment. Like choosing what to wear, learning to express ourselves should feel and be natural.

In society, we may sometimes learn to shut off and think it's wrong to express how we feel. But the way we view the world will always have implications on our health. There is a link between our emotions and our immune system and studies have shown that persistent exposure to high levels of anxiety and stress can adversely affect our physical health.

Blaming others doesn't deal with the root cause of why we feel anger, or why we carry guilt, but it can start to compromise our health in the longer term, if those things aren't dealt with. In order to heal and stay well, we need to be in control of our emotions and learn to stay in control of them.

MINDFUL THOUGHTS AND NEGATIVITY

Mindfulness is the practice of concentrating on our breathing and noticing how our body reacts in that moment. It is something we can do at any time; we don't need to be in a specific place to do it.

It is often difficult to try to change our attitudes around our realities, because our realities can sometimes be difficult to deal with. They may also take time to work through, particularly if we're dealing with, or continually living with negativity.

Being mindful helps control negativity and is one of the most important skills we can have. It is a mental state, achieved by focusing our awareness on the present moment, whilst acknowledging and accepting our thoughts and feelings without judgment.

It helps us learn how to detach from negative emotional thoughts, allowing us to create distance, so we can respond and react more positively around negative, or difficult situations.

What we should be aiming for is to observe our thoughts with little, or no reaction. Although it's not easy in the beginning, when mindfulness happens, we can create a more neutral situation for ourselves, so that we're not continually focusing on negativity.

Being mindful has many different positive benefits too. It helps reduce daily stress, depression and helps improve immunity. It also promotes healing.

REDUCING ANXIETY

Any thoughts around cultural beliefs can be the catalyst for holding on to negative emotions and struggling with anxiety. Those thoughts may also tie us into a set of beliefs that don't always form part of the spiritual process.

We may not question our path, or whether the path we're taking will help us on our inner personal journey, but tying ourselves into a belief system around culture may also produce mental clutter, because with any conditioning we may unconsciously continue to live other people's lives. It is important we use our emotions in ways that help us get the best out of our lives. Once we are able to get rid of the mental clutter, we can simplify our lives.

We need to bring empathy, tolerance and patience into the equation so they become part of us, and so that we can think about the spiritual invisible force that is around us. Being spiritual is a lifestyle choice that needs to be continually practiced. Spirituality keeps our lives real, and helps us to connect with our 'higher selves', when we learn to listen to that 'knowing little voice'. Feeling connected to something bigger can give us a sense of purpose and bring a sense of meaning into our lives.

When we can understand that everything around us is

aligned and we know that 'things happen for a reason', we can begin to take control of that which is within ourselves, and within our reach.

That knowing little voice may often bring the answers we need, and may also help reduce anxiety.

MINDFUL AWARENESS

Mindful awareness is less about technique and more about our willingness to be aware of what is going on around us and being in control of our thoughts.

Being mindful helps us cut down on low moods associated with living in the past, and not letting go of our experiences that can lead to depression.

Mindful awareness is something we can incorporate successfully into our lives, by paying attention to our daily activities, dealing with any issues we have, both past and current, and learning to mentally stay present.

CHAPTER 5

SPIRITUALITY: A WAY OF LIFE

'The smallest flower is a thought, a life answering to some feature of the Great Whole, of whom they have a persistent intuition.'

HONORÉ DE BALZAC

Spirituality is a way of life, a life that's full of meaning. It connects us to the universe; to something bigger than ourselves, to the order of the law. It follows in the formation and operation of the universe, resulting in positive emotions, acceptance, contentment and gratitude.

Spirituality gives us a purpose, it helps us think about the way we conduct ourselves in our everyday lives, it connects us to ourselves, to others and to nature.

Those who live a spiritual life put their emotional health first. Emotional health is about cultivating a positive state of mind, which helps us broaden our outlook.

Spirituality is a lifestyle choice that we can all benefit from, particularly when it becomes a way of life.

MY SPIRITUAL BELIEFS

Given my life experiences, I could be bitter and negative. However, instead of dwelling on the negative, I have chosen a more spiritual path for myself.

Spirituality is a road of self-discovery, recognising the deepest of values in the human spirit, as opposed to material or physical things, so that we can aspire to life in its simplest form, without negativity or complications.

Spirituality has helped me find understanding, in a way I was unaware of before. It is about inner peace and giving without needing to receive. I draw inspiration from the smallest of things and look for the lessons I am shown, even if those lessons don't always make sense at first. My beliefs help me focus away from my physical form and that helps me take away the stress.

I have days where my beliefs are put to the test, but I am drawn back like a magnet. My spiritual beliefs help me understand more of my experiences and why the life I've had was always meant for me.

LIVING A MINDFUL LIFE

We are connected to each other, to everything in nature,

and to everything in the universe. Therefore, living a mindful life is important. This is 'The Law of One, Truth that All is One'.

We are responsible for ourselves and each other. What we do to others, we do to ourselves, therefore, we should be mindful of our actions. We should continue to promote self-responsibility and accountability for ourselves and be mindful of what we put out there. We need to protect ourselves and others, and in doing so protect the universe, for us to survive. (Source: https://www.mind-your-reality. com)

Being mindful and living a mindful life means taking it upon ourselves to understand how the universe and universal truths work. When we work according to universal truths, our lives and our planet can work out for the better.

We may experience health, abundance and happiness when, through universal truths, we are able to master our thoughts, directing ourselves to the lives we want to live. It is important to work from a universal standpoint, to continue to put out good, for the greater good.

MENTAL FORTITUDE

Mental fortitude is our ability to focus on and execute solutions when faced with adverse or uncertain situations. It requires patience, exploration, creativity and execution. It is what is needed in difficult times.

When we can develop the mental fortitude necessary to stay strong in the face of adversity, we end the fear of being in it. When followed through, mental fortitude creates confidence; when you add confidence with mental fortitude, you create opportunities for change and success.

Define your goals and be clear about what they are, be sure your goals fit well with your values and beliefs. Weigh up all the details, look for solutions and have a plan in place. A true win in business or in life is one that is mutually beneficial to everyone involved.

With efficient procedures or the right ones in place, we can have necessary strategies to help us attain our goals. Don't worry about failing. Failing is necessary because it helps us understand what structures, or strategies are missing. Not all procedures will work effectively, and we may not always understand how to achieve, or attain our goals.

But mental fortitude comes about with stability. Once you have stability, it is easier to remain mentally tough. It is the stability of what we put in place that gives us something to lean or count on. It is not only stability we rely on.

Mental fortitude is our ability to focus on and successfully overcome our doubts, our worries, concerns and difficult situations. We need to be honest and have integrity. We need to take ownership for our mistakes and we need to be accountable.

Mentally strong people are not afraid to take a look at themselves, they're not afraid to examine where they have gone wrong, or where they can make improvements. It helps them to readily accept what is, without needing to question.

SETTING A POSITIVE TONE

As I mentioned in Chapter 4, every day we set the tone through our words, energy and actions, therefore, it's important to get the tone right.

What we say, how we behave, the energy we bring into our relationships, into each interaction are important, if we are to reach a desired outcome. We have the opportunity to set our tone positively.

When we set the tone, we establish a particular mindset. It establishes the way things will continue, through institutions, in the workplace and in school. It is important to set a positive tone as this can shape our mindset, our goals and our lives. We should acknowledge individuals, respect our differences, keep an open mind, be open and honest and use open communication with others.

The path to setting a positive tone needs to be intentional. We can gain self-insight, bring clarity on what we want to create, then can act in alignment with the vision we anticipate moving forward; a vision we wish to create.

FINDING INNER PEACE

Finding inner peace is about having self-acceptance. It comes through acceptance and being happy with ourselves. We shouldn't have to prove ourselves to every person we come into contact with.

But its path can be long or short, depending on whether

our personal inner conflicts are resolved. The more we understand other people's reasoning behind their actions, the more we understand them, the more we can have inner peace.

Practices such as Zen teach us to ask more questions, to understand everything we need to come to understand. The more questions we ask, the more we can understand.

Where religion may push specified behaviours and practices that define us, with Taoism you learn truth is what you discover for yourself on your own terms; and that everything is relative. Its teaching, although initially hard to grasp, is necessary in helping us to find inner peace. (Source: https://personaltao.com)

We have our own truths and we have the universal truths and combined they work well, as long as we continue to work in shaping those values. It reaches the point of acceptance where 'as you are' can become the answer for the majority of the questions we face.

OUR CARBON FOOTPRINT

Reducing our carbon footprint is important if we are going to stop damaging the planet and promote healing for the benefit of future generations.

There has been increasing recognition in recent years that the way food is produced and consumed is unsustainable and cutting down on meat and dairy products is the biggest way that we can reduce our environmental impact.

This is because meat and dairy production account for a disproportionate amount of land take, water consumption and greenhouse gas emissions.

We should all aim to reduce our carbon footprint, in an attempt to stop harming our ecosystem and contribute to tackling climate change. The widespread acknowledgement that animal products are responsible for many environmental problems confirms that reducing our consumption of animal products will deliver more environmental benefits than trying to buy sustainable meat and dairy.

Therefore, eating less livestock produce and more of a vegetable-based diet has the potential to make both us and the planet healthier. The suggestion is not that we should all become vegan overnight, rather moderate our meat consumption.

The planet relies on us all to reduce our carbon footprint. Scientists have been talking about this for many decades, but we're now only waking up to the realities of what is potentially irreversible environmental consequences, if we don't take climate change seriously and act on it now.

WE LIVE OUR KARMA

If you believe in karma, you know that however you choose to live your life, you may have to deal with karma. You may also know it as the law of cause and effect.

Karma is an opportunity for personal, emotional and

spiritual growth. Karma is energy, and the energy we create by an action needs to be returned. It cannot be avoided. Karma doesn't wait until we pass over to spirit. It is present in our daily lives. The energy created by our actions is stored within our memories and activated, sometimes straight away, sometimes later on, but always in this life.

Karma works by itself and chooses when it serves its response. We have no control over when that will happen, but karma is responsible for how we get to live our lives and how successful we can be.

Whatever happens to us, it is the direct result of karma being released. The more we act in accordance with how the universe expects us to act, the less suffering we will have.

Where karma is concerned, it is not that something happens *to* us, it is something that happens *for* us. In other words, we are responsible for what we get back. The decisions we make influence karma.

Making positive choices that concur with good practices can soften the intensity of situations resulting from returning karma. It is therefore important that we're conscious of the choices we make.

Ask yourself, do my choices serve only me? Who may be affected by them and where are my decisions coming from? Are they coming from me, or my higher ego?

It's important we give consideration to this and act in accordance with the 'karmic rules', so that we can live in harmony not only with ourselves, but also with others.

AT PEACE

We don't have to live on a deserted island, with no access to the world to have peace. Life doesn't work like that, but changing certain thoughts means we can work towards having a little more peace.

It is important we think about our emotional energy. We need to learn, to know that our surroundings and conditions respond to our vibration, or energetic field. Our vibration is based on what we think and feel. We call the shots on how we feel.

We're not in control of other people, we can only control our own response, so we need to direct our focus in the direction we want our focus to go. Although we may physically pick up on what is happening around us, we need to mentally and emotionally acknowledge what is happening in our everyday lives.

Instead of letting your conditions influence your mood, let your mood influence your conditions. We can't always stop what's happening around us, but we can concentrate on finding solutions, so that we stop focusing on negativity all the time. When it comes to another person's behaviour, whilst we cannot control how they might respond, we can hope they will do right by us.

It may not always be how others operate, but we should always choose to see a higher perspective. We can do that by maintaining our connection with the universe and understanding the forces at play and their bigger plan for us.

SEEING THE WHOLE

Always look at the whole. Without the benefit of seeing the whole, we may defend something without realising it is only part of what we need to understand.

We need to see things from both sides so that we don't miss something critical; an insight that shows us the whole. We should always view something in its entirety. It's our ability to look beyond the bigger picture that allows us an insight and understanding of the whole. It is not a vision, but an innate sense of knowing.

Tapping into and learning how to use our intuition is the basis for us 'really knowing' and we can never truly know without it. It's our intuition that helps us make decisions, a knowing that is based on instinctive feeling, rather than conscious knowing.

BEING OPEN AND TRANSPARENT

When we work in open and transparent ways, it means we are open to new ideas and thoughts. It also means we are open to new ways of working; open through communication, open to new people, and willing to listen to others without passing judgment.

Being open and transparent means we are more likely to engage people in dialogue, without drawing them into debate. Being open allows others to come into our conversations. When we are open, we're not afraid to say what we feel. We are able to consider other people's thoughts and opinions too.

Being open means we can hear our own voice, speak our truth and that helps us to think about things. Being open also allows us to be who we are, without pretending to be someone we're not. Being open can bring peace and adds transparency.

Being open and transparent allows us to work in a way that lets others see what we're doing. We are then more likely to discuss what we're doing with others, given we have nothing to hide.

Being transparent allows others to see what we are like as a person. With transparency, there's no façade, no thrills, no airs and graces, what you see is what you get and you're not afraid to show it.

It's a state of mind, a lifestyle choice that incorporates general behaviour and how we choose to behave.

SELF-COMPASSION

Having self-compassion isn't always easy to achieve, but is doable. We can extend compassion to ourselves in times when we feel insecure, or if we're generally suffering as a consequence of a past or present event.

We can learn self-compassion by being kinder to ourselves, being mindful and responsive to our thoughts, about our experiences, without beating ourselves up every time those thoughts come into our mind. Whether our mistakes lie with us, or with someone else, it's important we let go of the baggage: and this is where self-compassion comes in.

OUR EARLY INFLUENCES

As parents, it's important we maintain our own morality if our children are going to have a chance of being raised in a moral way. The more moral the parent, the more moral the child will be.

Do we take time to consciously think about our moral standing? We may stick with what we've learned in childhood, with what we know, but we may fail to think about how our actions may impact others in the longer-term.

A parent who is sensitive to other people's feelings and injustices can influence early moral development in their children. It's what we as parents should be striving for. It's important for family members, including extended family, or anyone looking after our children, to have a similar moral standing.

We should take the time to work things through, instead of leaving our parenting to chance, in the hope that our children turn out okay. We need to be empathetic, patient and tolerant in our approach to problems.

The right influences go a long way to help build strong foundations for children. But it isn't just down to parents; influences need to be uniform across the board. We should want to guide in a way that better helps children.

Our positive parenting approach can have positive influences on our children that not only make us better parents, but can, in the longer term, make us better people too.

PRACTISING MINDFULNESS

Mindfulness is a tool that has become helpful to mental health professionals. Cultivating mindfulness is a powerful practice in therapy.

If practised regularly, it is a tool that can help us understand, stay in control and deal with our emotions in a healthy way. Mindfulness allows us to change our daily habit responses, by enabling us to stand back so that we can choose how to act.

Therapists who practice mindfulness can have better outcomes with their patients. It has also been successful in treating many mental health struggles.

Mindfulness has been proven to help individuals suffering with bipolar and personality disorders. It has also been documented that mindfulness helps lessen recurring depression. Because mindfulness has been so successful, it has been integrated into clinical practice, with many therapists bringing meditation and other techniques into their practising methods.

When we are able to continue to focus our awareness in the present moment, we contribute to repairing cell damage, which can in turn extend our lives. If we understand how the mind works, we can be better equipped to understand our feelings, instead of allowing feelings to dictate our behaviour, or overpower us.

Also, when we are aware of what is happening in the moment, we can begin to recognise and learn how to handle our thoughts. Mindfulness helps us concentrate better, whilst reducing any conscious thoughts that tie us into upsetting situations and add to high stress levels.

Mindfulness allows us to observe our thoughts, feelings and senses objectively. It's important we learn to do this sensitively, particularly in the early stages of practising the technique, because it is easy to give up.

PERCEPTIONS AND RESPONSIBILITY

From a young age, we develop our identities through self-image and create perceptions of how we view our beliefs, ourselves and the world.

We genuinely believe we see the world realistically and act in rational ways. When our own thoughts and behaviour are challenged, or accusations are thrown at us, our self-image can take a knock and this stress means we may not take responsibility.

Stress may also arise when we attempt to have or hold two conflicting beliefs, ideas, opinions, or attitudes at the same time.

On the one hand we want clarity, but we may struggle

to get it and therefore fail to bring acceptance, or closure. While we tend to work things out as we go, that doesn't mean we will always have the right understanding, or indeed the understanding required to bring closure.

Our experiences may also create cognitive dissonance. When we make mistakes, or fail to look at the whole, or think outside the box, the gap between our self-image and our behaviour creates the 'cognitive dissonance', as we struggle with holding conflicting beliefs.

We can either admit we made a mistake and re-evaluate our thinking, or continue to justify our behaviour, so that our thinking is not in conflict with our self-image. When we continue to justify ourselves, we only evaluate our own understanding of things, rather than what is necessarily right. In this way we avoid taking responsibility for doing what is right.

EMOTIONS AND DECISIONS

As our emotions dictate some of the decisions we make, it is important not to rush in, or make permanent decisions, unless we are totally happy with them. To successfully do that, we need to be aware of how we feel in the moment.

Through the gut, our emotions interpret, appraise and justify our experiences. This triggers feelings that we become aware of, and respond to. The thoughts that are stored in our unconscious also form part of that scenario, although we won't always consciously be aware they are the driving force behind our decisions.

It is also the unconscious that deals with the negative experiences that resurface and become the driving force behind some of our decisions. With work on ourselves, when we're in touch with our emotions that are stored in our unconscious, we won't allow our emotions to dictate our moods, or our choices.

Making choices depends on our understanding and interpretation of how we're feeling at the time, therefore it is important we make decisions with clarity and check in on our emotions from time to time.

Situations are often temporary, but decisions can be permanent, therefore a fleeting moment around a mood that fits our emotions could soon make a decision more permanent. Always try to base your decision making on present thinking, and avoid being dictated by your past, or your emotions.

HOW WE REALLY FEEL

How we feel about ourselves can be a mirror image of how we feel about other people. From an early age, we may be conditioned to think and behave a certain way and therefore won't stop to question our feelings.

But, we need to look deep within ourselves to work out how we feel about life, about life generally and other people, and be sure to include ourselves in that equation. If through our upbringing we are more uninhibited, we can come to understand and learn to explore our feelings more.

It's important to tap into our feelings on an unconscious level, so that we can explore them further. This is because it is our unconscious thoughts that have the answers. Our unconscious thoughts tell us exactly what our issues are and how we feel.

MAKING THE LINK

Without making the link between the past and the present, our lives may never change and any help we get may have little, or no impact.

When we fail to understand the past or our past experiences, we leave the past behind without an understanding, and history may repeat itself. In those situations, we may fail to make the link, fail to deal with and let go of our experiences, therefore, unconsciously fail to move on.

As part of the healing process, we need to understand the life we've lived, then decide if the life we're living is the one we want to continue with, or one that we want to change.

CONNECTING EMOTIONALLY

Emotional connections are what bond partnerships, families and friends together.

An emotional connection is a bond, it is a link that

ties something or someone together through a bundle of subjective feelings, and a bond that, once formed, is very difficult to break. Without an emotional bond, we may make decisions by ourselves without consulting close ones, and may often work and deliberate any decisions, independent of anyone else.

We may also continue to remain distant, holding back on our thoughts and feelings and sharing very little, unconsciously making excuses as to why we haven't. It is not something we consciously think about. Growing up with emotional connections helps make life easier.

In most cases, it is only when we see how other people connect emotionally that we realise our own relationships are lacking those close connections.

BEING HONEST

Unless we are without truth because we're mentally incapable of recognising and telling the truth, we know if we're lying to ourselves; we know what our values are and whether we stand and live by them.

We need to be honest with ourselves and want to change. Having the desire to change comes with a discipline of its own. We can change and start being honest with ourselves, but not all of us may have that desire. Others may not think or accept they need to change.

When we're honest everything falls into place and even if it doesn't automatically, we should have fewer obstacles in our way. When we're not honest with ourselves we live a lie. Life can then become a treadmill and one of deceit.

In the long term, being honest with ourselves means life becomes less complicated. Issues that once seemed daunting can become easier; and we can be more in control, more gentle with ourselves and with others too.

CHANGING FOR SOMETHING BETTER

There is no point in change unless you're sure what you're going into is better than what you have now. Never let yourself unconsciously believe you can't change, or that you're not capable of change and that change is only for others.

Don't allow your past or your future to be limited by your circumstances. Stop telling yourself you can't change. Instead of being afraid of what might or could go wrong, think about the things that could go right.

Change happens when we change our mentality. Having the wrong mentality is the reason we can stay stuck; it's the reason we may not be comfortable with change and the reason why we may shy away from it. But change doesn't have to be drastic. Change can be small but significant steps to a better life.

The right change can lead us into a more peaceful mindset with people we choose to have in our life, but our convictions for change need to match our desires. We need to remain stalwart in our thinking, or we may never work through change, and may simply settle for the life we currently have.

SELF-DISCOVERY

The journey of self-discovery is about discovering our true selves. It is about discovering our beliefs, living by them and then finding our purpose.

Discovering things about ourselves means digging deep into our childhood, to reveal some of the experiences that have shaped us. Self-discovery helps us uncover our values; our truths, natural talents, abilities, capabilities, our passions and what inspires us. Then the things we discover may be transferred into other areas of our lives.

It is important to understand how to use what we discover about ourselves, in a way that not only helps us, but others too. Self-discovery should empower us to think about our lives in ways that allows for personal, emotional and spiritual growth.

Through self-discovery we can be more in control of our lives, which means we're less inclined to judge others, or accept another person's dogma. The more we understand ourselves, the more we can be mindful of how we do things, such as how much we eat, or how much exercise we take.

Self-discovery gives us a deeper understanding of our childhood, of ourselves, of our lives. Discovering things about ourselves can help us think about how we deal with and resolve our issues, and that is so important if we are to take control and move on with our lives.

OUR LESSONS

If you're fortunate enough to have supportive parents or carers, you can learn many lessons from them, but for some of us, the lessons we take from them may not always be positive and may therefore change how we see and do things.

Our fate is sealed the moment we're born, but it may take many years for us to understand how fate works. Depending on our experiences, we may be rather naïve in thinking our lives will change.

Our lessons aren't always the usual parent-child lessons about life. We often have to work those out on our own. I would have to work through my disability: not knowing I had cerebral palsy until I was forty-six and then finding out at fifty-six that I had autism, what having a physical disability meant mentally and emotionally, and understanding my symptoms, difficulties and challenges.

RIGHT AND WRONG

There are people who we may gravitate towards and who are moralistic. They continue to exhibit goodness, use right and wrong and show others how to exhibit both.

Unfortunately, we won't all share or exhibit the same morals, but morals are the most important thing we can have. They are what define us and sets us apart from others. Morals set a standard of their own that is both important and desirable, that when used correctly, hold us in high esteem by others.

Our lives should be based on our moral compass, one that guides us every day when making decisions. Morals are a reflection of who we are and our spirituality. It is part of what spirituality is. Without morality it would be difficult for our lives to work out how we want.

Morality allows us to direct empathy and compassion towards those that need it, and helps us distinguish right from wrong. It can help us become better people, leading better lives.

OUR SENSES AND BEING MINDFUL

Mindfulness is an art, brought about through our observations. For those of us who practise, taking note of our surroundings is something we continually do, always observing, always in touch with our environment, always taking note of the world around us.

It is our five senses of taste, sight, touch, smell and hearing, which we employ unconsciously, that enable us to experience the world around us. They're all powerful forces that aren't always registered in our consciousness, but they're definitely there. They affect our mind and play into our decisions, without us needing to consciously register them.

As we go about our daily lives, we may fail to pay attention and take note of our senses, all of which are part of our decision making process. We may ignore our senses without apportioning importance, or observing them. But they are our window to the world; we experience most of our lives through them.

Failing to consciously take note of how what's going on around us can affect our decision making, we may also misinterpret and misunderstand what's being pointed out through these deeper channels. It would make a difference to our quality of life if, through our senses, we were to consciously take note of our decisions.

To be consciously aware is to be mindful, not just merely to see, but to strive, to observe and to understand. Using our senses allows us to foster a greater awareness of interactions between our environment, ourselves and other people. Incorporating these can help us become more mindful about our decisions, and the way in which we determine our outcomes.

CHAPTER 6

THROUGH THE HEALING PROCESS

'Love the animals, love the plants, love everything.
If you love everything, you will perceive the divine
mystery in things. Once you perceive it, you will
begin to comprehend it better every day. And you
will come at last to love the whole world with an
all-embracing love.'

FYODOR DOSTOYEVSKY

For us to live our lives comfortably and with a little more
ease through the healing process, we should restore physical
and mental health. Our lifestyles and how we choose to
live our lives are very much the catalyst for that.

Self-awareness is the first step to any kind of healing,
creating, solving, and overcoming the things we deal
with. Once we're through the healing process, we may
also restore an expansion of our consciousness, and live

'presently', so that spiritually we understand who we are, and why we are here.

BACK TO BASICS

Go back to basics, embrace your fundamental principles and find joy in the little things. Be content with what you have, be comfortable in solitude, in quiet contemplation and just be happy in the moment.

We may create our struggles by attaching too much importance to our failings and disappointments, without thinking about what we can learn and take from them. It all starts with us. Disappointments and failings are lessons, it's important we learn from them, and move on. We should learn to remove what is no longer in alignment with our values.

When we learn to stay centred, when we create a life for ourselves around our values and live with integrity, we can see what is no longer in alignment. When we go back to basics, we can remove parts of our life that no longer serve us.

It could be a job, family, a living space, a partnership, anything you feel isn't right. You shouldn't have to explain yourself to others; if you are already having to explain yourself, then others don't understand you.

Think about your day, where you need to be and how much time you have. Start your day in the right frame of mind and at the right pace. When you go back to basics, imagine how much better you will feel; how much more understanding, tolerance, and patience you will have.

Be content with who and what you have and with your achievements. Stop striving to have and want more; prioritise your work balance and free up your energy so that you have time to think about the things you need, so that you can make your life better.

COPING WITH LIFE CHANGES

When something significant happens that has an impact on your life, it can become life changing; in fact, it can be anything that changes how you feel about someone, or something. Coping with life changes is something we all need to learn, and it can be a challenge.

Any form of change can take its toll on our mental health. It's easy to become fixated on the events we have no control over, but if we can stand back and look at those events around what I would call the bigger picture, we may find we have some control.

Check in with your feelings periodically, so you understand how you feel and make positive choices, so you can pinpoint any problems and set new goals. Focus on and practice self-compassion and positive self-reflection.

What you feel about yourself and how you see yourself can make a difference to your relationships and how you cope when situations arise. Lifestyle also plays a part in how you cope. Allow for physical wellness and emotional health and you should cope much better through life's changes.

FREEDOM TO CHOOSE

Without healing ourselves, we may never have the emotional freedom to choose. Freedom represents peace derived from a willingness to challenge our experiences and existence and how we choose to live.

Freedom to choose a different way to think. Freedom to see things the way they are, rather than the way we want them to be. Freedom to make a difference in a world where we're constantly being told how to live and how to be. Freedom to change the things we don't agree with.

In a world where there is fear, my website, The CP Diary, reins me in. My writing allows me the freedom to choose what I accept. It offers me an alternative point of view, it shows me an image of how my life can be changed, with words, thoughts and feelings that encourage understanding of how we may all live better lives.

Through insights, my blogs show my intuitive inner workings, which provide answers to uncertainties, so that we get to move away from them, healed and free, towards a more peaceful existence.

THE OTHER SIDE OF FEAR

The fear we feel is the side of life we live, but unless we work through that fear, we may never get beyond it.

What we have on the other side of fear is a better emotional space. On the other side of fear sits peace and tranquillity, living with less stress. It can bring about calm and understanding, and can give us hope.

The other side of fear is living the life we dreamed of. It is reaching out, understanding ourselves enough to want to give life a go. The other side of fear allows us to trust. It is a place that can help us reflect and look back on our experiences, in a way that brings new meaning and understanding.

The other side of fear is where opportunities lie and where a new uncluttered, uncomplicated life resides, and where we get to live a more peaceful life. Without taking our first steps, we may never know. We are responsible and need to be instrumental in putting ourselves into a good emotional space, and on the other side of fear.

A LIFE WITHOUT EGO

We know the ego is responsible for leading our reaction or response, for other people's actions directed towards us, and us towards others.

Understanding and having knowledge of our personality and character, and how it leads us to act, allows us to communicate and change our actions in more positive and appropriate ways. When we understand the ego and how it operates, we can understand why it's better to work without one.

The ego helps us distinguish what is occurring in our mind, from what is occurring in the external world.

It is perhaps the single most important function, because negotiating with the outside world requires us to perceive and understand it. That's fine to a point. We can grow through the ego, both mentally and physically, because it's there to initially help us understand and make sense of the world, but we shouldn't be completely reliant on it, because eventually it can start to work against us.

The ego works against us when we fail to pay attention to ourselves and continue to answer to it, but it's only when we venture away from the ego, overcoming the inherent resistance to separate ourselves from it, that we recognise there's a life beyond it, one not to be feared, but embraced.

Working without the ego allows us to see and understand that we can show being grateful and thankful through our own free will, through the universe. The universe doesn't look for appreciation, acknowledgment and compliments, and neither should we.

When we let go of the ego, we go beyond its perceptions, and can embrace our own. Without the ego, we can be selfless so that we support everyone and everything that exists around us, through things like understanding, respect, empathy, compassion, patience and tolerance.

Freeing ourselves from the ego can free us from aversion, dislikes, antipathy and opposition: these can be the source of our unhappiness and restlessness.

WHEN IT'S TIME TO LET GO

There is nothing wrong with caring; but expecting others to care because we care may not always work.

You will know when it's time not to care and time to let go when:

- The time and energy you're putting in isn't reciprocated
- You're trying too hard to make the relationship work
- You're growing apart
- Friends or family stop making you a better version of yourself
- You can't count on the other person
- You're being ignored
- You're dealing with abuse
- Others have a hidden agenda
- It's clear your issues are being ignored
- Others don't want to help, and don't have your back
- Relationships feel strained or difficult.

When friendships begin to feel too stressful, when everything about the friendship becomes a challenge and you know in your gut it's not working, it's time to walk away.

If you want to stop caring, it's time to make changes to your belief system. Not caring doesn't make you heartless, or mean-spirited, but rather it frees you from the burden of needing to please others, and not feel guilty about it.

Not everyone is worth your time, energy and support.

We usually do that at the cost of our own mental health. It's good to be honest with yourself. The truth is, you are the one that's worth your time, energy and support.

SAYING HOW THINGS ARE

Being open and transparent doesn't always reward us with brownie points from those who aren't, but it does mean we get to sit comfortably with our conscience.

Although being open and transparent may not always sit comfortably with others, we shouldn't have to accept another person's behaviour, if we feel it's inappropriate. It is important we're honest, and say how we feel.

If what we say was done with good intention but results in a negative reaction, the recipient should think about the reasons behind it, rather than them making what we said about us. Not saying how we feel may eventually create a rift.

Not being open may also stunt emotional and spiritual growth, and adversely affect our health. Not saying how we feel can create emotional distance, fall outs, arguments and secrecy between people and in relationships and can be the difference between staying well and becoming ill.

Saying how things are means we are being true to ourselves. To stay well, we need to be open, honest and transparent.

MAKING YOUR OWN DIFFERENCE

In 2009, I started my blog The CP Diary, and never having missed posting a daily blog, I still continue to blog today. I have moved on emotionally since those initial days.

Through writing I have discovered that even with trauma and the events we have no control over, we can still unlearn and relearn a new way to be. A good thing about the human brain is its ability to re-evaluate what it needs. We need to want to re-evaluate.

We also need to want to change things so we can move on from our past; we need to want to make a difference for ourselves and in our lives, and should stop feeling sorry for ourselves. If the life we're born into isn't the life we want, we have to want to change that too.

NOW IS THE TIME FOR CHANGE

Be aware of your feelings, never lose sight of how you feel. Never allow another person's version of what you feel to get the better of you.

If you've been through years of feeling guilty for things you didn't do, or didn't achieve, now is the time to change. It is never easy living with other people's decisions, and even harder when their decisions leave you with feelings of guilt that aren't yours to bear.

And if those same people are unable to take responsibility and continue to play the blame game, turning every discussion about how you feel into an argument, maybe then it's time to walk away.

Life is too short to spend your time with people who do very little for you, who think you are the problem and who leave you with more stress.

ACCEPTING

Since we are all the product of our individual upbringing, development, environment and experiences, we can feel differently about many issues. When we come to accept ourselves, unconditionally, we can learn to accept our upbringing and our experiences more, and can begin to feel more comfortable about those.

But acceptance doesn't just stop with us. The world would be very small and less diverse if we all thought the same things and had the same beliefs. We should learn to embrace each other through our different cultures and beliefs. Being open to other people's cultures and beliefs can bring about opportunities for us to learn and respect each other's similarities and values, as well as our differences.

These are the qualities that make us unique, but our uniqueness can also drive us apart. When we close our mind to the possibilities of learning about others, we close the door to tolerance, understanding and acceptance.

As long as we're open enough, our life can encompass and mirror the people around us, otherwise our world becomes even smaller. We need to learn to adapt, accept and respect what others have to say. In retrospect, even if we don't agree, we need to at least learn to respect.

LEARNING TO IDENTIFY

We should allow ourselves to make peace with ourselves, and identify with our past and present lives.

By learning to identify with our experiences and ourselves, by dealing with and coming to terms with parts of our experiences, we can begin to open our minds to life in its present form and all its future possibilities.

We can identify and learn more through understanding our past and present issues, and how best we can make the necessary changes. It is also important we learn how to deal with our issues. Failing to do so can interfere with our physical and emotional health.

Although our lives may continue to exist without us always knowing or being able to identify our issues, these may resurface later on.

If we have things we're holding on to that we don't deal with, we run the risk of inviting illness in. It is important we identify and talk about our issues.

BEING ENCOURAGED

For those who welcome it, the encouragement they receive never goes unnoticed. Even if we are encouraged and we are not feeling encouraged, it's easy to lose sight of those who are supporting us. It may only be that we realise it when we look back, once we have found resolution.

But being encouraged can help build self-esteem and self-belief, it can make us more determined, wanting to continue to do and give of our best. Encouragement with motivation inspires us to try when we fail, to dig deeper when we struggle, and to continue to strive when we're not always feeling up to it.

With encouragement, we can feel empowered. Empowered to take action and be productive, positive in our endeavours to have and achieve success. But it doesn't always follow that those who set out to encourage have received it themselves.

Often, those who go on to encourage have had difficult lives and therefore come to know the importance of what it means. No matter the life, those who manage to encourage know the importance of care and, because they care, they are able to encourage.

WE CAN LAMENT OR MOVE ON

We can cry about life, how things have worked out, where we are and what we've not achieved, or we can rationalise and work on the changes we need to make. There is no point in lamenting or dwelling over a lost life, on the things we couldn't change.

Often, it is only when we look back at our experiences

that we know there is nothing we could have changed, although the rest of the time we may continue to convince ourselves otherwise.

It is also important we accept our regrets, and although they can never change where we are, or how we got to where we are, regret is a life lived and that's okay. When we come to think about our lives, we may become angry and irritable, when we continue to convince ourselves we could or should have been able to change certain aspects of it, or made different choices.

We may spend years unconsciously convincing ourselves that where we are is our fault, and that is what keeps us fixated. The truth is that if we could have changed things, those things would have changed, we would be living a different life and we would be different people.

QUESTIONS AND CLARIFICATION

Asking questions gives us clarity. It's the simplest way of learning and it is effective too. Questions are also the best way for us to gain deeper insight. Questions inform, inspire, and they encourage healthy debate and discussion.

But questions may not always go down well either. It depends how the question is asked, who is answering your question and whether they're happy for you to ask. Since asking questions is the easiest way to absorb knowledge and it's important that we ask, why then do some of us stop asking questions, and why do some of us not even start?

If someone else asks the questions, it means we don't have to. Others may also assume they know the answers, so don't bother to ask, or they know the answers. They will usually remain steadfast in their assumptions, as they continue to cling to their beliefs.

There may be times when we're afraid to ask because asking questions may show us in a poor light, if others think our questions are inappropriate, or they don't agree. On the other hand, asking questions is a sign of strength and intelligence and allows us to follow through with conviction. Asking questions also brings clarification.

SEEING WITH NEW EYES

We may spend a lifetime looking at things in the same way, failing to see and learn new things. The Novelist Marcel Proust wrote, 'The real act of discovery consists not in finding new lands, but in seeing with new eyes.'

We don't have to discover new landscapes to create new discoveries, we simply need to change the way we look at and think about things, to see through new eyes.

We may take the things we have for granted, we may not stop to think about who and what is important, we may become jaded. We may be short-sighted in how we see our lives, each other, what we have, how we behave and how we could do better. As we go about our lives, we may fail to see the bigger picture, of what things mean and why we need to approach our lives differently.

We need to see what we see with a new set of eyes so that we can become more tolerant, more caring and more compassionate. We need a better, more balanced perspective. We need to see our lives differently; and the people in our lives differently. We need to appreciate life and what people bring to our relationships. We're all different, our differences need to be accepted.

Henry David Thoreau wrote, 'It's not what you look at that matters, it's what you see.' If we choose to see others through new eyes, we can behave differently towards them, which means we can get a better response.

WALK THE WALK

Spirituality dictates that however our life works out, we are responsible. If we don't change anything, then that is our responsibility too.

It is not enough to talk about our issues, replay the same messages without redressing those issues, and moving on from our experiences. Also, we need to think about and come to understand other people's part in our lives, where they may fit in and why we may not always be responsible; not everything that happens to us is about us.

As children we're not always equipped to understand our lives, and if we are, we're not always in a position to make any changes, but it's different for adults. If we want to change something we can, or we may just choose to talk about it.

It's not enough for us to talk the talk, we should also walk the walk. When we tie our actions to our words, we have the ability to make significant changes towards a better lifestyle and life.

STOP DRAWING COMPARISONS

We should stop comparing our show reel to other people's; their show reel isn't ours, so it would be wrong to draw direct comparisons.

Our lives may not start out 'perfectly', but when we compare, we may spend a lifetime drawing comparisons. Instead, we should start to believe in ourselves, in our abilities, strengthen our inner core, believe we're good enough and choose to distance ourselves from any negativity.

We also need to move away and move on from those who spend their lives undermining us, making us feel guilty for our experiences, how we feel, or for our insecurities.

It is because we don't stop to look at our lives, appreciate what we have, or who we have around us, that our insecurities may stay irrational and we may remain insecure. Insecure feelings on the inside usually mirror how we cope on the outside.

So, use reflection as a tool to think about your life. Begin to look at life from the outside in, as if you were looking at another person's life. Be honest about what you see and own what's yours.

Choose to deal with your experiences, keep what's yours

and let go of the rest. By looking at your issues objectively, you can begin to build new, sturdier foundations.

The more you work on your inner core, the more you will mentally and emotionally grow, the less insecure you will feel, the more confident you will become. When your inner core heals, your insecurities should lessen, and the need to make comparisons should stop.

USING MEDIATION

Although mediation is involved and refers to an intervention in a dispute to resolve disagreements, there is a different explanation that works in life too. Mediation is an intervention in a process or relationship, and can also work in families.

Not all families use mediation. Instead, they may offer an opinion, one which isn't always welcome or accepted. Mediation starts with each of us. When it comes to family and family dialogue, mediation should be continually used to bring understanding into a discussion, or opinion.

Without a reached understanding, instead of both parties offering an olive branch and using mediation to talk about how they feel, they may often be too quick to throw in the towel. No one is free of issues, it is how we deal with them that is important.

Mediation is the perfect tool to bring clarity and understanding and, when it's continually used, it can also help us through the healing process.

WE CAN'T GO BACK

'I can't go back to yesterday because I was a different person then.'

LEWIS CARROLL

If we were to go back, we wouldn't know what we know now. We grow mentally and emotionally through our experiences. Our lives would never have changed and the people in it would still be the same. It is only when times are difficult that we may search and wish we were in simpler times, but somewhere in our unconscious, we've already worked out that we're better off where we are.

It is important we learn to focus on the things that are holding us back, and not spend so much time thinking about, or living in the past. It may be that we haven't yet got off the starting block, but we need to deal with our past if we are to live presently, and be successful in our lives.

The mind may often plays tricks on us and things seem different when we look back. Sometimes we may forget to take the rose-coloured spectacles off when we begin to paint our lives and people more favourably than they were.

We may believe and see the good in people, in our circumstances and in the past, even if our experiences didn't play out like that. Sometimes it's as if the experiences didn't really happen to us, but to some earlier prototype of ourselves. We may convince ourselves they weren't our experiences, or maybe it's just that we don't want to believe they were.

THE ART OF NEGOTIATION

Successful communication begins with our ability to negotiate and find a way forward, and whilst some of us may think that means we're giving in, in the long term it can make us more emotionally and spiritually wise.

Negotiations strengthen our resolve and authority. It means we're mature enough to look beyond the tittle tattle that comes with arguments and disagreements, not always needing to be right, or having to have the last word.

All negotiations need working at. Although negotiating may seem difficult at first, it gets easier the more we practice, but it also depends on the person we're dealing with and our circumstances. It is a tool that shapes our behaviour and lives positively.

When it comes to any form of negotiation, it's all about respect. It is about mediation, it shows others we are open to listening whether those negotiations are between family, friends, or work colleagues.

If handled correctly, all negotiations can be a positive experience. It is important we are approachable and open to other people's viewpoint. Negotiating is a discussion, a talking point, and a chance to listen to someone else's viewpoint that isn't our own. All it takes is an open mind and a desire to listen.

CHOICES AND CONSEQUENCES

Experiencing the consequences of our choices is probably one of the hardest things we can do, but it is an effective way of shaping a person's character and behaviour.

When we choose and make choices, we acquire skills that shape our lives positively, as long as we continue to practise them. The lessons we fail to learn along the way will always have consequences.

Most of us should learn our lessons, some may fail to learn, and others may fail and wonder why, but whatever our lessons are, it is important we learn to take responsibility and be accountable for our choices and any subsequent consequences.

Sometimes not making good choices paves the way for us to become responsible and accountable, through our understanding of how and where we could have done things better. We learn more from our mistakes, more than we do from our successes.

Life's lessons can be a steep learning curve. It is important we learn to navigate our lives, but we should also learn that, for every choice we make, there will always be a consequence.

OWNING OUR INDISCRETIONS

We all have indiscretions, but where some of us will own up to ours, others may ignore theirs, still see themselves as perfect, and continue to point the finger.

Instead of apportioning blame, we need to accept we all have indiscretions and that we're not in fact perfect. Pointing the finger at someone because they're being honest won't help us in the longer term. Our indiscretions will always be our indiscretions, and owning up to what is rightfully ours can bring a more positive outcome. It is right to own our indiscretions: they are ours after all.

SEEK YOUR OWN APPROVAL

Life isn't about seeking other people's approval, instead it should be about working on our own approval and seeing things for ourselves. We shouldn't need anyone to tell us we're good enough.

If someone chooses to walk away, opting to physically remove themselves from your life, their actions say everything about them. They are not the kind of people you'll want to be around.

It is important we understand that other people's limitations are their own and have nothing to do with us. They may be withdrawing because of how they feel about themselves, their insecurities and worth. Our worth isn't based upon other people's acceptance of us. We don't need anyone's approval, but we do need our own.

THE VALUE OF LISTENING

The art of success isn't achieved by speaking, but by our ability to listen. While some people may be impressed by how well we speak, others will be more impressed by how well we listen. The best outcomes are often governed by knowledge and wisdom, and by our ability to intuitively listen.

Effective communicators are adept at reading between the lines. They possess the ability to listen to what's not being said and fill in the gaps that need to be filled. Often, we may be in such a rush to communicate what we have to say, instead of listening to others.

But the value of listening can be the difference between success and failure. Don't be fooled into thinking it's more important to be heard. Good communication is looking for understanding, before we look to be understood. When we fail to understand, we fail to be understood.

We need to listen, instead of wanting to be heard all the time. Constantly wanting to broadcast our message doesn't have the same result, as if we were to listen and engage in conversation. Good communication takes place through a conversation, not a lecture.

The best outcomes come from our ability to intuitively listen and concentrate on our listening. Putting our listening skills into practice can help us achieve success.

IN PURSUIT OF HAPPINESS

I believe seeing other people happy makes us question our own happiness. As a child, looking at how happy other people seemed made me realise how unhappy I was.

When we look at other people, unless we know them well, we may think they're happy, but what we think we're seeing isn't necessarily what we're really seeing; we can never truly know.

The reality is that we're not always happy. Every day we live with hope that we may come to feel differently about our lives; that certain elements of our lives will change. In the early years it is up to our parents or carer to help us put that right.

I now understand the correlation between my disabilities and my mental and emotional health and why being happy was something I needed to work on.

In the pursuit of happiness, it may take us many years to understand that it is our attitude towards what we deal with that needs to change, and that we need to take control.

A COMMON-SENSE APPROACH

A common-sense approach to what we deal with is common sense. It is being able to stand back and think about what we deal with; it's the voice in our head that tells us to listen. By listening to our thoughts, we are able to rationalise and do what makes common sense.

Most of what we deal with is common sense. When we are able to apply practical knowledge around situations that require further clarification, we use common sense. Common sense allows us to make judgments and for us to sensibly behave in practical ways.

When we apply common sense to our problems, we learn how to solve those problems. How we inspire ourselves to sort our problems out can make a difference to the final outcome.

In certain cases, the cause of our problems isn't always where the symptoms show up, but if we know how to fix the symptoms, we can fix the problem and that's where common sense comes in.

There is always a solution to every problem. It is sometimes our inability to understand the initial problem and how to fix it that causes our problems to continue. It is our intuitive thoughts, the little voice in our head, that allow us to fix and find solutions.

UPS AND DOWNS

We can't have ups without downs, a negative without a positive, a good without a bad.

Life is full of ups and downs, but if we have to deal with more downs than ups, we may struggle to bring ourselves back up again, and that may affect how long we're down.

When we are able to contribute to our lives and take control, and we have come through the healing process, we come to understand that life is equally balanced. Ups and downs are inevitable. Work and life balance are essential if we are to have more ups than downs.

TURNING OUR BACKS

The hard part is knowing when it's the right time to turn your back on someone or something. There are two trains of thought here: understanding why you're turning your back and when it's time to give up.

If someone is abusive and they're making you stressed and ill, then it's right to walk away. But walking away can often lead to feelings of guilt; there is no need to feel guilty. Unless someone who is abusive understands they need help, they may not accept help. Not everyone stops to understand their life and equates they may need help.

Turning our backs on someone or something isn't a decision that is taken lightly or easily, but one that is often necessary. It is part of the healing process.

SELF-INFLICTED LIMITATIONS

The way we see and interpret our lives through culture and society means we set our own limitations and that is what we unconsciously continue to do.

Our environment, what is expected of us and how we're expected to live can make us somewhat narrow-minded. By having rules that we are expected to live by, we are automatically imposing another person's boundaries on ourselves.

It is those boundaries that narrow our view of the world and the environment in which we live. Not only do those boundaries narrow our view, but they can also limit our course of action and the decisions we go on to make.

Most of us may live with self-inflicting limitations, until we are able to start thinking for ourselves. Some of us may wake up too late to do anything about it. Others may never wake up at all, continue to think their limitations are other people's fault, and carry on unconsciously blaming their lives on everyone else.

If we are prepared to take the blinkers off, or dip our toes, we should see more of how we *could* be living, as opposed to how we *are* living. How we get to a particular place isn't something we can always change, unless our circumstances change, or those changes are made earlier on, but time can often move our thinking on; we can always change where we go from there.

It may be that when we look back, or we hit rock bottom, that we begin to see patterns emerging of how limited our perceptions are, and that can sometimes bring change.

A SIMPLER EXISTENCE

It's hard to imagine living life in the slow lane given our busy lives, but wanting to lead a simple existence means it could happen. A simpler existence means a slower pace of life and less stress.

Slowing down means feeling happier and more relaxed in ourselves, which means we can start to connect more with our emotions. A simpler existence not only makes us more interested, but can also make us more interesting too. It allows us to look at and notice the little things, the things we didn't notice before.

A simpler existence can bring us closer to our inner core, uncovering our flaws, faults and strengths, which are no longer hidden beneath the layers of accumulated distraction, clutter and junk.

The following tips may help:

CLARITY

When we are able to bring clarity into our life, it means we can begin to see who and what is important. Clarity can also help us to see and understand our experiences better.

GRATITUDE

Having gratitude can help improve health and well-being. We have a lot in our lives that we may have gratitude for, but it's often difficult to see when we're dealing with stress, and stressful situations.

DECLUTTER

Physically we are surrounded by clutter. Our homes are filled with clutter. When we take away some of the material clutter, we should want for less in other areas of our lives.

GENEROSITY, EMPATHY AND PATIENCE

When we realise that we need less than we have, we have more to give. Embracing simplicity means we can make intelligible decisions about how to best serve our lives and help others who need our help. Generosity, empathy and patience incorporate all that we come to expect from living the simple life.

HEALTH

When we're more mindful we can bring awareness to all aspects of our lives. Managing a simple life can help bring about an emotional awareness so we also become more aware of what affects our physical health. Simplifying our issues is synonymous with a simple existence.

THE IMPORTANCE OF RELAXATION

We should probably think more about relaxation so that we at least try to bring some form of relaxation into our day.

We may often use relaxation as a last resort, when we're made to slow down because we're feeling ill.

The 'fight or flight' response, as it is known, is often brought about by stress and stressful circumstances, and is difficult to avoid. When it comes to handling situations that are stressful, chemicals are automatically released into the bloodstream to prepare us for them. Once the stressful situation has passed, the body naturally returns to its normal state, prior to the fight or flight response.

Daily pressures can continue to create stress, but what matters is how we deal with those pressures, and how we deal with stress.

A little stress isn't bad for our health, but constant stress can begin to compromise it. We need to find time to relax. Relaxing gives the body a chance to repair and heal on a cellular level, so that if we ever get into fight or flight mode again, we're fully prepared for those eventualities.

Relaxation helps with renewed energy, gives us a better quality of sleep, better physical health, greater emotional balance. It also helps with improved concentration, increased energy levels and enhanced creativity. When we're more relaxed, we're better equipped to deal with stress.

So, learn to focus on what you can control and let go of what you know you can't. As they say 'Rome wasn't built in a day'; prioritise your 'to do list' so that you do the important things first, and get those out of the way.

To reduce stress, relaxation should be incorporated into our daily lives, as part of a healthy lifestyle. Self-care is an important element of helping us to relax and unwind, so try to plan ahead to avoid cramming things in, and look at any personal changes you think you can make.

Also, take down time, listen to music, go for a walk and take nature in, read a book, meditate, or sit outside in the garden and take time to relax.

DIFFICULT PEOPLE

We may spend our lives trying to make and put things right with difficult people, and adapting because we feel we have little choice. Difficult people we have a connection with may draw themselves to us because they know they can be difficult, and because we aim to please.

Difficult people may project their feelings onto us as if their feelings are our own. They may also project their anger onto us, fail to take responsibility and continue to pass responsibility on to us. After a while, if it is allowed to continue, we may start to believe we are the ones who are difficult.

Difficult people may project their feelings onto us because we're too afraid to say something or walk away, and also because we let them. Where we feel we need to put things right, we may continue to defend and justify ourselves, because it's all we've known and what we've always done.

But we need to be clear on what belongs to us. We shouldn't let difficult people think we need to justify ourselves, or own what doesn't belong to us. We're not responsible for how other people make us feel and we may end up bending over backwards in endless attempts to please, if we let them.

Instead, we should stop trying to please and physically walk away. When it comes to family, if we can't walk away, then we should distance ourselves temporarily and come back in when they stop being difficult, and we are happy to do so.

ARE WE REALLY HAPPY?

I was once asked the question about what makes me happy and I truthfully couldn't give a straight answer without 'going around the houses'.

From my experiences (and without putting a total damper on things), if you've lived with trauma, it is often difficult to own being happy. In spiritual terms, it took me many years to understand what it meant and to know that true happiness comes from the soul. It is what our soul has or hasn't had. If the soul continues to be nurtured, we can feel happy.

Happiness isn't something you just have. Stress can add to how you feel and unless you are able to correct what is wrong, inwardly you may never feel happy.

When the soul and our life has continually been conditioned, it is that conditioning that stops us addressing feelings around being happy. It is important to dig deep, for us try to pinpoint our unhappiness, so that we take away any stress, and surround ourselves with people who we know are good for us, and who want to make a difference.

If we don't feel happy in our soul, we probably haven't experienced true happiness, because everything we feel outwardly comes from the soul.

WHY WE MUSTN'T BLAME

Things that happen to us in childhood are usually as a consequence of someone else's actions, which if unaddressed can leave us less than able to cope with our lives.

It is possible to change early patterns by recognising our mindset traits and working towards changing the way we think, avoiding situations that promote emotional reactions, or patterns of reaction.

The thoughts we have about other people are usually a symptom of how we feel about ourselves. Blaming others is the true reality of how we feel about ourselves, we just don't see or get it. Blaming others who were never responsible for us highlights our own inadequacies and that's when we may become the victim.

We can choose to stay where we are, or we can empower ourselves by learning to change our pattern and mindset. We should stop seeing other people as the problem, and look at and deal with our own issues. Blaming others won't help us, or change our circumstances.

We can still learn to feel good about ourselves, by working on changing the way we feel and think, without pressing the self-destruct button, and looking for others to blame.

THE IMPORTANCE OF PATIENCE

How many of us lose our patience because we haven't got time? We're too busy making things a priority instead of making the people in our lives a priority; we're choosing to focus on the wrong things.

The world is moving quickly and, whilst we're keeping pace, others aren't always keeping pace with us. Also, when we're feeling anxious, concerned or worried about something we have less patience to listen. Do we see ourselves as being impatient, or do we think others are being difficult?

Impatient people want things done yesterday. They don't waste time in getting things done, but they forget to enjoy the experience that goes with it. When it comes to people, patience is important, because not everyone may get something the first time.

We may be impatient at times, but patience is something we should all try to nurture and cultivate. We should challenge ourselves to understand that all things happen in good time and for good reason.

Being patient is a key component of being happy. It is important to nurture relationships through patience, as all relationships need time and patience. Once we've mastered it, we should go on to replicate patience in other areas of our life.

SELF-RIGHTEOUS

Someone with self-righteous tendencies may display moral superiority, derived from their beliefs, affiliations or actions, which they believe are of greater virtue than others.

As a consequence, they may be intolerant of the opinions and behaviour of others. Their morally superior approach to their lives and towards others may make it difficult for us to like, or mediate with them.

Those who are self-righteous tend to have an attitude where they continually believe they are right, no matter what others say. But it shouldn't be about being right or wrong, it should be about being open to life and differing opinions, so we can see what's beyond our four walls and limitations.

We become self-righteous when we're too moralistic and intolerant of other people's opinions, when we choose not to be open, or discuss our opinions and why our views differ. Being self-righteous can make us impose our will on others. When we get into the habit of competing with others over our beliefs, unable to relate to people with different views, then we limit ourselves to life within our own four walls.

Throughout our lives we have many conditions imposed on us, we may also copy much of what we see.

Intuitively knowing something doesn't always make us self-righteous, but it does make us knowledgeable.

A BAD ATTITUDE

It doesn't matter what we say, or how kind, compassionate or conciliatory we are towards other people, there will always be someone who unconsciously thinks it acceptable to have a bad attitude.

People who have a bad attitude usually assume there is something wrong with other people, but never with themselves. Any problem they have is usually down to someone else. They're not willing to improve themselves, or change how they are.

Those people may be generally uncaring, inconsiderate and apathetic about how other people feel. But there is hope. Through the healing process, people can change certain aspects of themselves and their behaviour.

These are my affirmations that I use to reinforce positivity:

'I have trust in myself and choose to change positively. I am capable of change. I am confident I can change. I choose to change.'

THE VALUE OF POSITIVE EMOTIONS

When we live through things that we wouldn't want others

to experience, we know and understand the beneficial psychological effects of talking about how we feel.

Psychologists have researched into negative emotions and negative effects and how these bring about anger, stress and depression. If a condition like depression is allowed to continue, it can signal the presence of a psychological disorder.

As children, we may not always be aware of just how important our emotions are, and why being positive is an important part of that. As adults, as long as we continue to think about and choose to see our lives positively, those positives can bring about possibilities we didn't think were possible.

It's important we learn to cultivate and nurture our emotions, but we should also deal with our issues, because they can emotionally hurt us if we're not at peace with ourselves, or them. Being loved, feeling content and satisfied can all enhance our ability to adapt and allow for resilience.

Positive emotions can also enhance our ability to problem solve and infuse negative situations with positive meaning: it's that which facilitates us bouncing back. We cannot think about cultivating positivity until we deal with the issues that potentially cause things like stress, anger and depression.

The value of positive emotions, which are now more widely understood, are part of mental health and mental health issues. When we radiate positivity, we attract it back.

POSITIVE EMOTIONAL PRACTICES

To be able to deal with our emotions, we have to stay in control of our thoughts, feelings and behaviour. When we are in control of our emotions, we are likely to feel better about what we deal with and should therefore be able to handle our issues and ourselves better.

Having spent a life in contemplation from a young age, I have learned how to see and put my problems into perspective.

My own rules are:

- Say what you feel. This is so important and is the catalyst to positive emotional health
- Turn off your TV, computer, mobile phone or laptop periodically, or at least an hour before bed and listen to music, read a book, or have a conversation
- Go to bed early. A healthy sleep pattern and a good night's sleep helps the body refuel and allows the mind to rest
- Connect with yourself and take 'me time' regularly
- Try to eat a balanced diet
- Try to stop carrying issues. Emotionally, it takes more energy to carry an issue than it does to address one
- Take responsibility for yourself and your issues, but don't take responsibility for issues that don't belong to you
- If you struggle to talk about your emotions, write them down

- Stop sitting on the fence, and avoiding confrontations. Confrontations can happen whether you try to avoid them or not
- Finally, work on your self-esteem and deal with any confidence issues. Avoid negative family situations and choose positive friends. Also, try to keep yourself busy so you can begin to feel and think more positively.

The more you are able to carve out a lifestyle that is both calm and peaceful, the more focused you can be. The more focused you are, the more you can begin to deal with negative issues and thoughts positively.

THE IMPORTANCE OF TALKING

Growing up and struggling through school, I wanted to know why I found it enormously difficult to learn, to mentally and emotionally adjust into school life. I wanted to know why I had a bad leg and foot and why they looked different to my right one.

Although mental health issues weren't openly spoken about when I was a child, there's no doubt that families were of course still aware of physical, mental and emotional issues that needed to be addressed. When it comes to mental health, the importance of talking cannot be stressed enough.

Nowadays we have a broader understanding of mental health and the importance of talking, but misconceptions still exist, and mental health issues remain prevalent.

A report by Time to Change estimates that 65% of young people with mental illness have faced stigma from their friends, with 50% experiencing stigma from their parents. The same report highlights the effects this can have on our mental health, as well as on the rest of our lives.

Thirty per cent said mental health had prevented them applying for, or taking up a university place. Fifty per cent talked about the fear of negative reactions preventing them from applying for jobs, or the stigma they had received. A further 28% said other people's reactions had made them want to give up on life. (Source: https://www.time-to-change.org.uk/)

We need to talk about how we feel. When others don't talk, we also learn not to talk. Being able to say how you feel is one step further away from stress, anxiety, depression and mental illness. Share your personal experiences, talk about how you feel. Encourage others to talk about their emotions and what they may be dealing with.

We can all help to make a society where we have control over our mental health, and we don't have to feel bad about things. By simply having a conversation, we can help take away the stigma of mental health.

THE NEED FOR PATIENCE

We live in a world where many people expect instant gratification. In the blink of an eye we have information at our fingertips, through the internet.

Technological advances are positive, but the flip side of that is we continue to expect things at our fingertips. And whilst we've created a niche for ourselves through the latest technology, we often unconsciously think we can have the same in our relationships.

We can't have instant gratification in our relationships, and should continue to work at them. It is important relationships are cultivated and nurtured so they include things like tolerance, empathy and understanding.

We need to look at how we can be more patient, kind and understanding, and think about who and what matters to us most in our lives. It is also important that we think about and change the way we communicate with each other.

WE CHOOSE WHAT WE SEE

Perception doesn't record reality, perception records what we want to see in the way we want to see it. Our mind constructs how we choose to see the world.

Perceptions depend on our assumptions of what we think and how we see things. We all have a different take on what we see, around which we build our realities. The things we believe are real are governed by our perceptions.

Some of the things that we perceive as real are not real to someone else looking at the same scenario. But, because not everyone is mentally or emotionally ready to change, they may be reluctant to change what they know and see.

It's the way we think that changes what and how we perceive things, which may explain why we can go through life judging others by their previous actions or behaviour, instead of how they are now. They could have changed, and yet we may still judge by how we remember them.

Through the healing process, we all have the opportunity to grow into the people we are destined to become. As children, we are conditioned by our parents, our circumstances, and by our environment, including our peers. As adults, we can choose how we then want to live, by making the necessary changes. For those who struggle to emotionally move on with their lives, they may have a hard time accepting others who have.

We may either choose to hold on to the old character traits we had as a child, or we work to change how we live our lives and then choose what we want to see. For it to successfully work, others need to mentally attune themselves to the new us.

THE BEST OF INTENTIONS

It would be wonderful to think we live in a world where we all have the best of intentions, where we do things because we're well-meaning and we want the best for each other.

Sadly, life doesn't work like that and another person's intentions may not always be as honourable as our own. Or maybe it's not even as black and white as that. We may start with good intent, but fail to act or follow those through.

Either way, good intentions are meaningless unless they are followed through in a way that benefits or helps others. Individually, our wants and needs are different, so our well-meaning will be different, also.

Our purposes and how we manifest them, are just as important as how our intentions are received by others. There is a well-known saying 'do to others as you would have them do to you' but, in reality, we often expect others to treat us better than we treat them.

Not everyone has our best interests, or the best objectives in mind. For example, a narcissist wants the best treatment from others, but won't or can't accept they need to treat others with good intentions. A hidden agenda and insecurities can play a big part in people's good intentions.

However we are able to manage it, it is equally important to try and give of our best, because when we're no longer here, we will be remembered by our deeds, whether they were good, or not.

A LETTER TO MYSELF

I have always had the ability to think about 'things'; if I was to write myself a letter about my 'spiritual and healing journey', it would go something like this:

You have come through your life with composure. I love how you have managed to weather the storm; where you could have given up you didn't, but instead you chose to understand all that has happened.

It wasn't difficult to see and understand your struggles. You were always a kind, caring, compassionate and pleasing child, but the mental and emotional side of any disability can bring about feelings of anger. Even through your struggles, when you weren't angry, you still continued to please, now helping others through your blog, The CP Diary.

You know that if you were to rewind the clock, you would have still taken this path with your writing and website. The events of your life have led you to this place. Even if you had a name for your disability in the early years, your experiences would have still been the same. You would have continued to struggle in school with your mental and emotional health.

Your diagnoses would have given you something to hold on to, but since everyone's brain damage with cerebral palsy and autism is different, you would have got no further in understanding how your symptoms around your mental and emotional difficulties presented. You've had to further research all of that yourself, and although you know your education was important and needed to be addressed, you also know that with help you could have fared better in school.

Your spiritual beliefs are your inner strength and they have enabled you to work through your spiritual and healing journey with compassion. Even though you hated looking at yourself in the mirror, as a small child you still knew something was wrong, not just because of your leg shortening, your drop foot, or your lack of muscle tone on your left side, but because you knew your eyes looked different and your facial expressions were flat. Although you couldn't pinpoint what that meant, every time you looked in the mirror you knew the girl staring back at you didn't look right.

It would take you another ten years, from your initial cerebral palsy diagnosis in 2009, to find out you also had autism at the age of fifty-six, and that explains your mental and emotional struggles, learning difficulties and how you look.

Although a turning point around your mental and emotional struggles, particularly in school, this was yet another difficulty, because it came at such a late age. It's good that after all these years you have been able to piece together the reasons behind your mental and emotional struggles.

The way you write and what you write is who you are, and both are testament to how you live your life. It would have been easier for you to have ignored your disabilities, but you didn't. Instead you moved forward, starting your blog after your cerebral palsy diagnosis. Seven years later, your first book helped you explore your disabilities for the first time, and then taking your spiritual and healing journey through to your second book.

Your life was never going to be easy; your emotional strength, spirituality and healing are testament to how far you have grown, and to how far you have come.

You know that without your blog, you could never have written about your thoughts and feelings, or been able to explore in detail exactly what your disabilities meant: that was meant to happen.

Without your books, you would never have understanding around your disabilities, or known what you know now; you also could never have come through the spiritual and healing process in the way you have. You now have understanding, clarity, acceptance and closure.

Although it has taken you years to come through the healing process, your spirituality has been with you since very early on, and that has enveloped you in its arms and it continues to carry you through. It has been instrumental in your cerebral palsy, spiritual and healing journey. You have come through the healing process a more balanced and happier person.

What matters is that you accept the importance of what you have achieved. You have come a long way since your initial diagnosis. Your strength of character shines through your writing, always seeking out the truth in a fair and a conciliatory way. You can stand tall and be proud.

Your unique talent defines you. Your ability to write and turn bad into good, negative into positive, bitter into sweet and rough into smooth; to come through in a way that continues to help others in their own journey, that is your legacy.

I am immensely proud of you.

MY EMOTIONAL GROWTH

Having a disability with my specific brain damage meant I didn't have access to the usual emotional thought patterns and ability to grow normally, mentally and emotionally.

It would take me many years to learn about myself in my relationships, and that hasn't been easy. Waking up for the first time to my diagnoses, but not knowing anything about my symptoms and how I mentally and emotionally presented, meant I had to learn everything from scratch, including my neurological difficulties and how those difficulties play out in my daily life.

It is through emotional growth that we learn about our likes and dislikes, what irritates us, what makes us happy, what makes us sad, and what makes us, us. We become independent thinkers, and ready for the challenge any new relationship brings. Having grown, we're comfortable with the concept and the challenge of moving on.

Going into any relationship and not knowing anything about yourself means you end up learning about yourself in the relationship and that can often bring about a different thinking. Through the other side of what we have to deal with, we are not the same people.

My ideals and aspirations have changed. I am not only older and more informed, coming through those late experiences, but having brought myself to an altogether different place and having grown through learning about myself in the process, I am also spiritually, mentally and emotionally different.

I live with morality based on my spiritual beliefs and now have less tolerance and patience for the petty stuff.

SELF-DEVELOPMENT

Self-development is something we may be aware of and, if it's something we're not doing, we probably need to, but not everyone may work on their self-development.

It has everything to do with our core values, beliefs and lifestyle and it promotes emotional and spiritual growth. If we persevere for long enough, personal growth can lead to new opportunities, but we need to be mentally and emotionally prepared to look for and seek out those opportunities.

Self-development allows us to take our first steps, for us to learn about ourselves and then deal with our issues. When continually used, it can help us learn new skills and improve ourselves. Self-development encourages potential, can help make us more focused and efficient. It can also help with motivation, helping us change our attitude and perceptions.

Without self-development we may stagnate, but with it, it gives us a better quality of life that leads us to seek out potential success. If continued, self-development helps us become a better version of ourselves.

BECOMING BETTER INDIVIDUALS

We are answerable and ultimately accountable for what we

say. If we understand that we're responsible for everything we say and do earth side of life, when our life is revealed to us on our passing, more of us may have chosen to become better individuals.

Unfortunately, we don't always stop to think about our lives until it is too late.

BRINGING CLOSURE

With the right understanding, it is possible to turn our backs and bring closure on some of the experiences that continue to hurt us.

When we ask, perhaps our loved ones may not answer our questions, perhaps they may answer them but only give answers they think we need to hear, or perhaps they may avoid accepting responsibility, so we are unable to bring closure. But we can bring closure, with or without them accepting responsibility.

Although it's not always easy to do, it is something we need, if we are going to have peace. It is also not something anyone else can help us with. It may be that we have to find closure on our experiences by ourselves, putting things right, without those who have wronged us putting it right for us. Not everyone admits they did wrong, but they should want to admit it for themselves.

That said, through the conscience, we can still bring closure. The conscience is the soul reflecting upon itself as it allows us to make moral self-evaluations on our experiences. The conscience has an innate ability to sense right and wrong, and contemplate the actions of others.

When we can distinguish our own moral compass and the moral compass of another person objectively through our conscience, we can equate and understand the way our lives turn out, without having to carry someone else's guilt.

It becomes a vicious circle, because without peace we can never have closure, and without closure we can never have peace, but it is possible to have both. With a new understanding of how the conscience works, we can have new perceptions on the way we feel about our experiences. When we think about a particular experience, and about someone without feeling dread, we know we have come to terms with it and have closure.

FEEL WHAT YOU FEEL

We may hide behind different guises. We're good at disguising and hiding emotional pain that comes from negative beliefs brought about by a particular situation, or person. These different guises are fear induced.

We're afraid that if we show vulnerability, we may let our guard down and that can make us look weak. But this is not altogether true, because when we open up and show others we're dealing with our emotions, we become emotionally strong. Showing others our vulnerable side shows them just how open, sensitive and strong we are.

It is important to explore our feelings and learn how

to feel what we feel. We tend to internalise and analyse our feelings, but we don't feel them. That's because it's sometimes too painful.

Perhaps our feelings are associated with a sense of loss, a sense of failure; a sense of pride, or a sense of guilt; or perhaps we're afraid we may lose control if we reveal our feelings, or we're vulnerable and won't cope with the pain.

What we think matters, but what we feel matters more, but as long as those thoughts don't ignite discord and disharmony, we should be okay. We need to be aware that when we ignore our feelings, we're inviting illness in.

We should be responsive to what we feel. We need to understand and own those feelings. Without this, we may never be able to cultivate positive relationships, empathy, compassion or tolerance.

Being able to understand and feel our emotions helps with empathy, compassion and tolerance through the healing process. It also helps us go on to change how we see our lives and manage our relationships.

OWNING OUR MISTAKES

Where we fail to own or admit to our mistakes, people may see through our behaviour and our avoidance of responsibility.

Perhaps people seeing through our behaviour is because they know where we're at and what we're doing and they want us to be more accountable. On our part, being less accountable means we're less likely to own up to our mistakes.

A lot of how we are stems from childhood. Starting from a young age, we develop an identity that is made up of our beliefs and how we see ourselves. Everything we learn in childhood we take into our adult lives. When children fail to say sorry, it's often because their behaviour is being ignored. The more accepting of ourselves we are, the more likely we are to want to own up to our responsibilities, and admit that we made a mistake.

Life would be sweeter and easier if we did. There would be less room for disagreements, fall outs and those inevitable pregnant pauses over the mistakes we don't own up to.

LIFE IS WHAT WE CHOOSE

Life is what we make it. But choosing to be insular, not acting in other people's interest, as well as our own, not being a team player, can stop us from being part of 'something' that has the potential to be good.

When we fail to see what's in front of us, and continue to dwell on how we'd like things to be, the picture we paint in our heads may be different to our realities. We need to accept, embrace and contribute to our lives positively and in the interest of others, for us to know that what we put in is what we will get back.

We may think the grass is greener and that our lives will

be better elsewhere, that what we have isn't what we want. But if we ever chose another path, we'd probably find the grass was just the same. We would still have to deal with ourselves, our experiences and our issues.

The reality is that we are where we are supposed to be. Our experiences and issues are ours to have; life is what and how we make it, therefore, it's important we don't make our experiences, issues and our lives about everyone else.

UNDERSTANDING THE REASONING

We need to understand the reasoning behind another person's actions, and to understand why they would choose to behave a certain way. No one should be on the receiving end of another person's bad behaviour.

Whatever their reason, it's not okay, especially when everyone can make a difference and they simply choose not to. Of course, no one's infallible, but for those of us on the receiving end of another person's actions, it's important we understand why, so that what happens doesn't consume our every waking thought.

It doesn't get people off the hook, or make what they've done right, they will still be accountable and responsible for their actions, after all 'what goes around comes around'. But what it can do, is stop us taking in another person's negativity, because that can make us ill.

AN OPEN MIND

Having an open mind is important, because it allows us to understand what's happening in our reality, so that we can make sense of the world. It opens our mind to what other people have to say, whether or not we choose to accept what they say.

For me, having an open mind is part of being spiritually and emotionally independent, being able to make my own choices. Being independent gives me freedom of choice, freedom to choose my beliefs and freedom to choose how I incorporate those beliefs into my realities.

Having an open mind helps me embrace new beliefs, so that I can learn and change my perceptions on how I view and deal with what's going on in my life.

When we can make sense of the world, we are more likely to want to take the appropriate action to live more fulfilling lives. An open mind allows us to be willing to think about other people's beliefs, even if we don't agree with them.

To have an open mind, we need to make a distinction between our beliefs and the truth. Once we have made the distinction, we're more likely to keep an open mind, even if our thoughts differ from others.

HAPPY, RELAXED AND CALM

People with happy dispositions can have periods of low moods, disappointments and problems in the same way as those with unhappy dispositions. The only difference is they may adapt more easily, and their disappointments and low moods may be dealt with more swiftly.

Happy people tend to have a relaxed and calm demeanour about them, regardless of what they have to deal with. They are usually more content in themselves and know to take the rough with the smooth; they are ready for what comes their way.

They are aware of how they feel. They can take things in their stride and accept the inevitable. They tend not to panic and know that as their low moods come, they can go. They are more generally accepting of their feelings and aren't particularly fazed by what they deal with. They get on with putting their world right.

The reality is that all our experiences are etched on our souls, so if our souls are tormented, then so are we. That said, we can all work at being happy, we need to put in the effort, so that we become a better version of ourselves.

We can all work on change. Our beliefs and experiences can help shape our ability to stay focused and calm, which in turn, shapes our personality and our ability to deal with our issues. It's important we learn not to fight our feelings and accept that we have them.

Feelings are there for a reason, it is important we acknowledge and deal with them, and learn to go with the flow, because this helps us to remain calm and at ease. By working on ourselves, through emotional and spiritual growth, we can be happy, relaxed and calm. How we choose to look at life is how we will deal with life.

INEVITABILITY OF CHANGE

We initiate certain changes that we're okay with, but when change is imposed on us by others, we're not always okay about it.

Certain changes like moving to a new house, or changing jobs can be exciting, but whilst we're initiating those changes, we may still feel apprehension and concern over whether it will work out okay. We tend to reconcile, so our choices fit in with our wants and needs at that time.

But what about change that is imposed on us by other people or circumstances? Are those experiences likely to feel different? It would be easy to feel different about them. In some ways, change that we're not prepared for or happy with, can make us feel fearful, even frightened. It may also depend on how we feel about having change imposed on us.

In circumstances where we deal with unexpected change, we may find ourselves resisting change altogether. We're hesitant because we're not sure and resist anything we're not sure about. It's perfectly normal and comes with the territory.

But without making ourselves stronger and changing our perceptions, we may never work through the inevitability of change around our perceptions. Whilst change is hard, it becomes inevitable as nothing ever stays the same.

WAYS OF BUILDING RESILIENCE

Resilience helps with life's journey. It doesn't matter whether we need it to help us cope with a serious illness, or the death of a loved one, it is resilience that gets us through. It helps us pave the way for a more calm and peaceful existence.

HOW WE BUILD RESILIENCE

- Change your attitude so that you interpret and respond to events positively
- Continue to work on your emotional health. Learn to build on your strengths, and how you see yourself. They are all great tools
- Learn to accept the things you cannot change. With new experiences you can learn new things that expand your mind and build resilience
- Continue to identify and incorporate your own strategies for building resilience
- Always remain optimistic about situations, and let go of the things you have no control over.

BUILDING TRUST

As we grow up, trust isn't something we are all afforded. The relationship between a parent and child, if handled appropriately and correctly by the adult, lays the foundations for trust between them, and allows the child to develop their personality.

Children need to have trust, and to know they are being cared for. Trust brings about certainty where there is none, it is a practice of faith. Trust is what you carry within yourself. Building trust takes time, it is the backbone to all relationships; it is a bond that parents should initiate, one that parents should nurture for their children. Trust allows us to form healthy relationship attachments.

It helps a child grow up to become confident, particularly in social settings. The relationship between a parent and child is one that should nurture the child's emotional, social and physical development.

Children need trust to help positively promote their mental and emotional development. Trust and support can help them go on to live their lives with confidence.

CARE ABOUT THOSE WHO CARE

We may sometimes care about those who don't care about themselves, and who struggle to care about us. We may often tiptoe through life doing things to please others, partly because it's expected, and because we don't want to rock the boat.

It's natural for us to care, and behave in ways that continue to tie us into other people's lives. Our actions are moulded by how we think others may perceive us, and that can stop us from living our lives. We care too much about what others think.

But living our life caring what other people think can become exhausting. It is okay to care, but we should try to care about those who care about us. It's important to stop living up to other people's expectations, or living other people's lives. People will judge and have an opinion, no matter what you do.

Instead, simplify your life. Live by your own set of values, because that will dictate who you allow in your life and who you will let go of. Ignore comments from those who judge, they will judge anyway.

It is the people who don't judge or pass an opinion unless you ask for one and who will be there for you during your worst times; they are the people you should choose to focus on. Care about those who care about you.

RELATIONSHIPS AND BEING JUDGED

There is a saying, 'it's better to come from a broken home than to live in one.' We shouldn't feel guilty about walking away from relationships, if it means we're supporting our mental and emotional well-being.

We may find it hard to walk away because we fear judgement from others for leaving a relationship, but whichever way you sugarcoat difficulties, if you're looking at abuse, it is right to walk away. Abuse in any form is never okay.

FATE AND DESTINY

'Destiny is a word that implies an ending: a destination to one's life. When two people were "destined for each other", they've given in to a notion that the journey is complete. The best definition to fate that I've heard is that "fate is what happens". In other words, fate is reality.'

WIKIPEDIA

Fate is reality, it's what happens. Fate is what we endure, until something happens to change the status quo. Destiny is different. Destiny implies an ending, a destination to somewhere, that our journey will be complete. Destiny is a journey we have control over and our destiny changes when we change. When we change our circumstances, that becomes our destiny.

But whether you believe in fate or destiny, you can get to change the ending. Something you're born into isn't something that will continue indefinitely. Just because you start out one way, doesn't mean your life has to continue that way.

But we should be determined to change, to move on. We should remain stalwart in our determination to change and to transform our circumstances. What we change is the start of a new destination and that becomes fate, a new reality that's different to the old one.

RECOGNISING YOUR OWN QUALITIES

Do you ever think about what you like about yourself, or what is good about you? Do you pay yourself compliments on your achievements but still wish you had done more, or instead do you compliment others on what they achieve and ignore yourself?

Did your parents compliment you? Did they acknowledge your achievements or the achievements of your siblings? Do you find it difficult to give out compliments because you were never paid one?

If we are praised as children, as adults we should find it easier to praise and be praised. If not, we might manage to pay compliments to our children, to other people's children, but remain reluctant to pay one to ourselves.

If you're unable to recognise your own qualities, or you can't bring yourself to pay compliments, remember these issues aren't about you, and you can always set to change them. What happens to us can be as a consequence of someone else's actions and words.

Try writing down all the qualities you know you have, and acknowledge your achievements. Your issues maybe as a consequence of your family's inability to praise, compliment and support you, to allow you to grow and become who you were supposed to become. You can change it for yourself, and for your children.

Through new understandings and new eyes, you can change how you see yourself and your life. The life we're born into isn't the life we have to continue to live. Although we initially may not always be aware, or be able to change certain things, nothing stays the same, circumstances do inevitably change, and we can change. We should be mentally and emotionally prepared.

A good affirmation to use: *'I've got this, and I can do this.'*

BEING YOURSELF

I have heard the saying 'be yourself' so many times before. As easy as it is to say, in reality it isn't something we always know how to do.

To work it out, we should make a start by looking at ourselves, our lives and our decisions. We need to learn everything about ourselves, get to know ourselves, find out what makes us, us. We need to make our own decisions.

We also need to allow ourselves to emotionally and spiritually grow. When we continue to allow others to define us, it means we may never be ourselves; we won't grow.

Instead, we need to accept our mistakes, deal with them and move on. We also need to stop worrying about how others may perceive us. We can't please everyone, so logic tells us there is no point in trying.

Always having to be on your guard because of something you've said only serves to make you more guarded. By learning to let go, you can use your own considerations as a filter. Also, learn to be open and honest about yourself, and try not to beat yourself up over the things you have failed at. Failure doesn't always need to be seen as a negative experience.

As we grow, there may also be things we don't like about ourselves physically, but it can be good for us to learn to like those parts of ourselves too, because only then can we unconditionally learn to love ourselves.

MAKING MYSELF STRONGER

Blogging on my website and writing my books have helped make me mentally and emotionally stronger. Being able to talk about my experiences in a self-contained and safe place has changed the way I see myself and my life.

Although I have encountered bitter experiences, my writing has enabled me to unravel my thoughts, so I am now able to see my life more clearly and positively. I have chosen to let go of the things that held me back. Living inside my head for as many years as I have, I see and think differently now. Making myself stronger has made my life easier.

Understanding ourselves and understanding our mental and emotional struggles allows us to come to terms with our experiences, and life. When it comes to our emotional struggles, it is not always about us, it's often about others who may inflict their issues and emotional pain on us. I see and think differently now about my disabilities, and looking at my life in the whole, I no longer struggle to look back.

SPIRITUALITY AS A WAY OF LIFE

Being spiritual is a way of life, it is a lifestyle choice that brings about many positive benefits to our health and well-being, and our lives.

Spirituality is not a religion; it has nothing to do with religion. It includes a sense of connection to something bigger than ourselves. It is a principled way of life that encourages our well-being and positivity. It inspires and helps us find our inner voice, so that we can inspire, and be inspired.

Everyone's spiritual path is unique to them. Interpretation of spirituality can and does differ; it can be used as a coping mechanism for stress. Spirituality has also been linked to positive feelings, of being able to handle stress better, better health, and greater psychological well-being. Spirituality is about integrity and integrity is character. Integrity, together with our inner voice, encourages us to want to do what is right for ourselves, for our family and others.

Spirituality allows us to live by our values and conscience, so that we can live better lives, united through a common cause to care and look after each other.

COPING WITH COVID

It is because I have autism that I have particularly struggled to cope with the Covid-19 pandemic. As the world

267

continues to live alongside the virus, I have struggled to come to terms with the pandemic. I have struggled to fit into the new 'normal' and that scares me, although I know I can't change it and I mustn't continue to stress about it.

It has reinforced the fragility of our mental and emotional health, and now, more than ever, we should take care and be responsible for ourselves. The life we had before the pandemic isn't the life we have now. Times have changed and we need to change with them.

Life before the pandemic has gone, and through our understanding and response to the virus, we need to find an acceptance. We need to learn how to get on with our lives, whilst we live alongside it. We need to be okay with it, while we also continue to be mindful of it; to change the things we can change and stop worrying about the things we can't.

COVID-19, OUR IMPACT

It is important to understand from a universal standpoint everything there is to know about the Covid-19 virus and why now is not the time to become complacent and revert full steam ahead back to our old lives.

We need to think about and change our lifestyles to fit into this 'new world' and embrace the change that has already happened.

The United Nations has declared that the pandemic was caused by human interactions and our impact on the natural environment. (Source: https://pjmedia.com) Therefore, it is important to change our behaviour, so that we can save the planet for future generations and conserve and protect the planet's threatened habitats.

We have all seen the impacts of global warming on the planet, people, animals and their habitats. Year on year, global warming statistics show an alarming rate of change. The gradual heating of the Earth and climate change doesn't just lead to the destruction of habitats, according to the UN, it has contributed to circumstances in which the Covid-19 virus has been able to thrive.

LIVING WITH THE PANDEMIC

As a general rule, I look at things positively to see how I can feel better about what I deal with and what I need to overcome. I am now coming to terms with and feeling more comfortable about living through the Covid-19 pandemic.

In the early months, I struggled to cope with hearing about what the effects of the pandemic were. It scared me so much that at times I couldn't sleep or eat, but thankfully I had my writing and blog to keep me company and to focus on.

Months on and I am aware that none of us can change what we are living through, but we can change how we see the pandemic and how we function.

It was difficult in the beginning, but thankfully now I'm feeling more comfortable, so that when I think about the pandemic, I no longer panic.

COVID-19, IT'S TIME TO CHANGE

There are moments in history that are etched in our memories forever. The world grinding to a halt in response to the pandemic is undoubtedly going to be one, and it is in times like these that we need to change how we think about the world and about our place in it.

It is easy to feel invincible in a modern society where we're living longer than ever before, and yet, despite all the technological advancements of the last century, we are still powerless in the face of floods, fires, earthquakes and viruses. What is now clear is that Covid-19 is a story of humanity's ever-increasingly harmful interaction with all other living things on this planet.

It's not enough for us to sit back and watch, we need to be proactive, and interventionist, to redress the balance of our impact on the environment. While it's easy to concentrate on the constant stream of bad news we are exposed to, there is a much larger opportunity to transform the way we think about our place in the world, as one of the many living creatures that inhabit this planet.

As the impact of human activity slowed during global lockdowns, we experienced the natural world reacting to the slow-down in all sorts of positive ways with improved air quality in cities and fish returning to waterways, hitherto devoid of life. Not only are these reminders of the impact humans have on the world, but also of the natural world's ability to rebound and our ability to change our behaviour when we absolutely must.

As individuals we need to share collective responsibility and readjust our priorities. The pandemic will undoubtedly leave an enduring mark on all of us as we contemplate the fragility of life, the flaws in our globalised economies, our relationships with all living things and, ultimately, our ability to see a different future. The natural world needs our help and we need to work together as we all inhabit the same planet.

The social impacts of the pandemic on our general well-being and our mental health are far reaching and should also not be forgotten. They have reinforced how important it is for us to continue to work on ourselves.

MY UNDERSTANDING

Spirituality has allowed me to incorporate contemplative practices that change how I see and live my life. Spirituality is considered to be a path toward self-actualisation. It is a guide that allows us to direct our attention to a specific, often inward-looking reflection that, if practiced well, gives us the answers we need.

Through centuries of spiritual practices, spiritualists continue to use contemplative practices to increase their self-awareness, to offer compassion and empathy, as well as being able to quieten the mind through spiritual contemplation.

Spiritual people are gracious. They are happy to extend what they know to help others, expressing gratitude. Spirituality encourages positivity, empathy, compassion, respect and tolerance, for us to be caring, for us to think about and put others first, but still not forgetting about ourselves.

Spiritual people flourish. They tend to be happier and they want for less, meaning their lives are less cluttered. They understand integrity, honesty and friendships, being open and what's important to them and what they want out of life.

Spirituality promotes self-healing. Those who practice spirituality concentrate on their internal values and work on becoming better people. They have meaning and a purpose to their lives. Many people follow spirituality as a means to find the essence of their true selves. Others use it as a desire to have a connection with their higher consciousness.

Whatever your reasoning for finding spirituality, spirituality can bring you understanding and peace. It can also enhance your view of the world, your life and of each other.

Spirituality has and always will be my life. It has given me hope, it has allowed me to work through my disabilities with grace, to learn about myself and to understand the bigger picture.

It has got me through some very tough years and has helped me come to terms with my disabilities and I wouldn't be without it. It has got me through the healing process.

MY FINAL THOUGHTS

Without having lived my life, I know that I wouldn't have come through the spiritual or healing process in the way I have.

It's not to say I wouldn't have gone down the spiritual path because there was always a curiosity there, but from an early age, I always knew my life was going to be difficult.

I have learned spirituality can lead to a balanced and centred life. Although it's not always easy to understand the concept of how spirituality works, just changing one thing so you can start on the spiritual path can change how you see and live your life.

Living a spiritual life isn't a challenge, it is our lack of understanding of spirituality that makes it a challenge, and the lifestyles we choose that take us away from a spiritual path.

Being spiritual allows us to be better people, living better, more peaceful and simpler lives.

Where the world needs more respect, empathy, compassion and tolerance, spirituality has these in abundance, but we have to want to incorporate a spriritual way into our everyday lives.

I hope that by the time you get to the end of this book, it is something you may think about, and want to embrace for yourself.

ACKNOWLEDGEMENTS

To Brad, for taking my book journeys with me and for the wonderful support and encouragement, for the early mornings and late nights of proofreading... thank you.

To Dan and Claudia, you continue to be my inspiration.

To Mum, your words opened the door to a changed life and I haven't looked back.

Lastly to Heather and the rest of the fabulous publishing team at RedDoor Press, for making my books a reality.

ABOUT THE AUTHOR

Ilana's cerebral palsy diagnosis was hidden from her until the age of forty-six. That diagnosis was a life-changing moment that allowed Ilana to look at her life experiences differently. Months after her diagnosis, she set up her website *The CP Diary*. Ilana spends her days writing and blogging about things that contribute to her health and well-being. She uses her experiences to write, bringing clarity into her life. She writes about health and well-being, advocating positivity, empathy and understanding through her blog, and across social media. Ilana, who is passionate about the environment and is an animal advocate, lives with her husband and their much-loved cat, in Yorkshire. When she is not writing, Ilana enjoys days out exploring the beautiful North Yorkshire countryside. This is her second book.

Join the conversation at
www.thecpdiary.com

ALSO BY ILANA ESTELLE

ILANA ESTELLE

CEREBRAL PALSY

A STORY

Finding the Calm
After the Storm

INTRODUCTION

MY STORY

What is it like living with cerebral palsy? I cannot truly answer that question, as for forty-six years of my life I never knew that's what I had. It was only in March 2009 that I was finally diagnosed with cerebral palsy.

I was born the second of premature twins. How did I feel as a child, growing up? Those times were enormously difficult for me. I was an angry child living in the depths of despair. Some days I felt isolated, angry and misunderstood. Other days I felt frustrated and alone.

I was out of touch with reality because I had no idea what I was dealing with. I was also out of touch with my thoughts, primarily because I had no understanding around my physical, mental and emotional issues. We didn't talk about my disability: my issues were never brought up unless I talked about them, then they were dismissed as if the condition didn't exist. But it did.

I know there was a diagnosis of cerebral palsy at the age of two, because I now have a letter in my possession for a referral to a specialist as there were concerns about my balance. When my twin was beginning to crawl, I would fall, try to get up, then fall again. It was never something I could control, but how I wished I could. My mum noticed I was falling, instead of crawling. My dad, on the other hand, was not unduly concerned, and said everything would be OK.

Growing up, I felt different for all the wrong reasons. I knew there were things I struggled with. I didn't like being angry, although every now and again my kind side would appear, and I would somehow be able to separate the two issues. There was Ilana with the condition, and there was the 'real me'.

A few years later I remember telling myself that I was glad to be me. To this day I don't know why I said it; I just knew I wasn't always unhappy being me. I also knew that deep down I wasn't a bad child. I was a child with a disability I knew nothing about, and emotional issues that weren't being addressed or going away.

Although I spent a lot of my formative years being angry, it would take forty-nine years for my father to say that I was the most kind, caring and considerate of his children. In order to earn his acceptance on a disability I didn't know I had, I found myself conforming more than any of my siblings.

In fairness to my mum, she tried to deal with me but couldn't cope. She was always singling me out to do my exercises, at a time when my siblings were doing something they wanted to do. I became irritated with this, and nine times out of ten I would fight the system and become angry at the injustice of it all.

My mum would tell me I couldn't have a pretty face without a pretty leg. I never made the correlation because I didn't know what was wrong and because nothing was ever explained to me.

In my yearly consultations, questions were never asked about my condition and how the condition presented, men- tally, emotionally or physically, which I began to think a little odd. With my notes now in front of me, I know the original diagnosis of spastic monoparesis at the age of two and a half wasn't correct, because I have two limbs affected not one, and my leg isn't spastic. This diagnosis was unknown to me at the time, and for most of my adult life.

Since my diagnosis at the age of forty-six, I have had to work everything out for myself, to bring my symptoms and the right diagnosis together. I have little muscle tone from the hip to the ankle on my left side. I also have a 'foot drop' and my leg on my left side is three-quarters of an inch shorter than my right side. This explains why, as a child, I would drag my leg and walk toe-heel all the time. The specialist never raised the fact that because of my 'foot drop' (a paralysis or muscular weakness which makes it difficult to lift the front part of the toes and foot) I would experience bunion issues. Years later I had a bunion removed.

Going out for walks my father would often walk behind me, telling me to stop dragging my leg and pick my foot up; I suspect he knew that was impossible for me to do. As time went by, and as a consequence of him picking me up on those things, I struggled with walking in and out of rooms, for fear of people watching me.

I hated looking at myself in the mirror and hated having to do exercises even more. When I was standing straight, I was lopsided because I had a leg length difference. When I spoke to my mum about it, she would reaffirm, 'I couldn't have a pretty face without a pretty leg.' With hindsight, without her realising, she confirmed she was aware of my diagnosis.

When I wore skirts, the lack of muscle tone in my left leg was visible, so people stared. I would limp and trip up when I got tired. I hated that. I also hated that I walked toe-heel, that I dragged my leg and I couldn't pick my foot up. I hated even more that I was being picked on for something I couldn't change and that was becoming an issue. I hated that I struggled to fit into shoes and that when I did manage to get shoes to fit, they wore differently. I was also upset at having to wear a heel lift underneath my shoe to compensate for my leg length difference, and that eventually I had to have shoes made for me that made my foot look even more deformed.

I also struggled with my handwriting. I hated not being able to write properly, or spontaneously, made worse if I had to write in front of someone. For example, writing a cheque at a till was difficult, writing anything in fact. I continue to struggle to write and with the way I form my letters.

Since my cerebral palsy diagnosis, my neurologist has explained that the part of the brain that controls my motor skills functions is also affected, so that explains the problem with my handwriting.

As a consequence of my parents wanting me to be the same as my siblings, my issues lay dormant for many years, as I continued to physically, mentally and emotionally struggle.

I lacked and craved mental and emotional support. It didn't help that I was born in the 1960s, a decade in which disability was commonly brushed under the carpet.

For fifteen years of my life I went to physiotherapy once a week, the Athletic Institute for exercises in May once a year, and the hospital in February once a year. All those visits seemed to eat into my childhood. As a result of my struggles, I lived a somewhat insular life, hiding a lot of my issues behind a timid façade.

But not knowing what my condition was always gave me a quiet confidence that tomorrow was another day and that things would change, and I would get better. To this day, I believe it was precisely because I had no idea of what I was dealing with: that gave me hope.

Find out more about RedDoor
Press and sign up to our
newsletter to hear about our
latest releases, author events,
exciting **competitions**
and more at

reddoorpress.co.uk

YOU CAN ALSO FOLLOW US:

 @RedDoorBooks

 Facebook.com/RedDoorPress

 @RedDoorBooks